CW01426281

Susanna Scott lives in a seaside town on the Yorkshire Coast. She loves her family, gardening, reading, writing books – and tap-dancing! Robin Hood and the Wolfshead Tree is her first children's book.

Also by Susanna Scott, for adults -
The Gypsy Caravan.
The Winterfell Stone.

Susanna Scott @yorkshirecoastwriter
on Facebook

Robin Hood

and the

WOLFSHEAD TREE

Susanna Scott

For my wonderful grandchildren,
with love.

In the middle of a wood on the edge of the market town of Buckton stood a large tree. An enormous tree. It stood way above the other trees round it. It was called the Wolfshead Tree because outlaws were also called Wolf's-heads and hundreds of years ago, they used the tree as a hiding place. Sometimes they had done nothing but steal a loaf of bread so their family didn't starve - or stopped one of the Sheriff's men mistreating one of the townspeople. The Sheriff wanted to put them all in jail – or worse…

This oak tree was so big and wide that anyone in need of shelter would be able to creep in the hole at the bottom to hide and nobody would find them. They would be safe.

In ancient times, forest covered much of Britain before people chopped the trees down. Many hundreds of years ago, this wood, which the people of Buckton called Robbers' Wood, was much bigger and covered all the fields around it where the farmer now grew wheat and barley. Many years ago the forests stretched from Sherwood Forest near Nottingham, up to Barnsdale in Yorkshire - and people on the run from the Sheriff roamed from one forest to the other. Robbers' Wood was just a small part of it.

It was said that a Roman road ran through it and if you walked there on a night, you could hear the Roman soldiers marching on their way to battle.

It was also said that, even now, if you stayed very quiet on a summer's day- you could hear the laughter of the outlaws in the wood and the thud of an arrow as it was shot into one of the trees. The legends also spoke of Woodland Spirits living there.

Yet for centuries, Robbers' Wood had simply been a wonderful place for generations of children to play; to climb trees, to paddle in the stream, to make dens – and to hide in the trunk of the Wolfshead tree.

If you were to climb to the top of this tree, you would see over all the fields, the church, the town – and you would see the farmhouse where Max Cooper lived with his family.

CHAPTER 1

'Will you stop laughing and just help me down from here?' shouted Max Cooper to his two friends who were rolling about on the ground making snorting sounds and clutching their stomachs. The sight of Max hanging upside down just above the men's heads, hidden only by the leaves on the Wolfshead Tree, had just been so funny. Jake climbed up and released his foot from the ivy it had caught up in, then Max tried to turn himself the right way up but slid very ungracefully down the tree to end with a painful bump on the damp moss. He rubbed his backside while trying to ignore his best friends, who were desperately trying not to laugh again.

'Well, that's it then!'

He bent forwards and his floppy blond hair fell over his eyes.

'No more woods, no more stream, no more dens, no… Nothing.'

Max looked up at his friends, a look of absolute despair on his face. Suddenly, they felt as downcast as Max was. They didn't feel like laughing now.

'He won't be allowed to do it.' ventured Ethan.

'You can't just go cutting trees down these days,' said Jake knowledgably, 'you need special permission.'

'You heard him though, he's got "friends in high places" and there's no doubt that he can talk them into it.' Max jumped up agitatedly and began pacing around the tree, 'This wood has been our special place for years and for our parents before us. They are not going to take it from us without a fight. I'd give anything – *anything* – to wipe that stupid smirk off his face. I wish we could save the woods and beat that idiot once and for all.'

Max stopped pacing and drew himself up to his full height, which was quite tall for a twelve-year-old.

'We need help.' he declared.

'From who?' asked Ethan.

There was a noise from nearby which made them all jump guiltily. The sound came nearer and Max's hair fell in his eyes again as he recognised the sound and put his head in his hands.

'Maa-ax!'

'I hear the sweet tones of your sister's voice calling you.' sniggered Ethan.

'Maa-ax!' bellowed the voice again.

Less than a minute later despite all three of them keeping extremely quiet and trying not to breathe, she found them.

'Aha!' she shouted triumphantly, 'You're in trouble!'

Cait, Max's sister, had their little brother Joe with her, his favourite hat pulled down so far over his eyes that he kept tripping over tree roots.

'What have I done now?' sighed Max

'You're late for lunch and Auntie Bess and Uncle Ferg are already sat at the table waiting. Mum's furious.' she finished with a happy smile.

Max realised then that he had promised to be back, washed and ready, over an hour ago and threw apologetic looks at his friends as he walked towards Cait. Everyone turned to go apart from Joe who was pulling on Cait's hand and trying to get to the tree.

'What's that?' said Joe looking puzzled.

'What's what? asked Max.

'That thing there,' he squealed excitedly, 'coming out of that hole in the tree. It looks like a…'

'Never mind that now,' said Cait, pulling him away, 'come on, we're late.'

'Meet you here, usual time tomorrow' Max shouted as he dashed off with Cait, only stopping occasionally to pick Joe up as he tripped over a root in the ground. Joe was too busy trying to look back at the Wolfshead Tree. He was sure he had seen something else there, something that shone in the sun between the branches. He wanted to go back but knew there was no chance with Cait pulling him at a hundred miles an hour.

Their house was not too far from the edge of the woods. In fact it was the last house you saw before you got to the trees. It was a very old farmhouse perched on top of a slope looking down over the nearby market town of Buckton. Max had timed it before and it took him three minutes to get to the wood from their house and another three to get to their meeting place by the Wolfshead Tree.

Dad was at the door and made a tutting noise when he saw them but didn't look too angry all the same. Their cousins, the Terrible Twins, Evie and Eira rushed to greet him happily, throwing themselves round his legs so that he could hardly walk. Bess and Ferg were smiling too as they greeted Max but mum took one look at the muddy, windswept apparition in front of her and shouted,

'Upstairs! Wash! Now!'

You can see where Cait gets it from, thought Max.

*

The next morning, Max woke early after a restless night thinking about their discovery. They had known something was going on in their woods because there were men in yellow jackets with 'Cheetingham Ltd' on their backs. They were walking up and down, measuring the ground and marking trees. It was the school summer holidays and Max and his friends were spending all their time in the woods. They had been in their well-hidden willow tree den near the stream when they had heard voices nearby. They slowly moved themselves so that they could make out who it was. Suddenly the voices were very close. Ethan and Jake had run back to the den but Max ran on to the Wolfshead Tree and quickly climbed up it to hide in its branches.

'We'll get rid of this little lot, no problem, especially that monster of a tree that looks like it's going to fall down anyway as it's so old.' The voice had come from Mr Cheetingham, the local squire who owned the Manor near the wood, as they walked towards where Max was hidden.

'But isn't it common land belonging to everyone? Won't you have a problem with the locals? asked another voice.

'There are ways and means round these problems man.' brayed Cheetingham, 'I've got friends in high places. It's not what you know but who you know. I own the manor and therefore the land. The common land thing is only hearsay and nobody would dispute my ownership as it's in black and white on documents. Besides, we'll have these trees chopped down before anyone has even seen the real plans for the complex. I told you – friends in high places'

Max didn't know what they were building but he did know that this wood and the stream that ran through it was a playground and a special place for the children from the market town below it. His parents had played there and their parents before them. Local people took walks through the wood and picnicked there and getting rid of the wood or even part of it was just not right. It was only quite a small wood, as woods go, but when you were in the middle of it, you couldn't see anything but trees and it seemed like a magical place.

It was Max's grandfather who had told him about the 'Wolfshead Tree' as it was always known although sometimes it was just the Big Tree. You might have thought that many of the trees in a wood would be big but when you came across the Wolfshead Tree, there was no mistaking it. The trunk was about six feet wide with a hole at the bottom that a few children could shelter in if it was cold or rainy. It had huge gnarled branches and holes all around it up to the top. The two largest branches looked like arms and when they had their leaves on, they protected the children from the wind and rain when they stood underneath it. Max wasn't really very brave and his parents' friends always called him shy, which really annoyed him but there and then he made his mind up that something should be done.

'No,' thought Max defiantly 'they can't cut it down.' and he pulled on some clothes and set off early for Robbers' Wood.

'Wait for me-ee.' Cait's sweet little voice came drifting across the field sounding like a donkey with a sore throat. He stopped, sighed and turned around to see his sister who was two years younger than him, struggling to catch up with him. Even further behind was six-year-old Joe, his hat falling over his eyes again. Max sighed again and turned back round, quickly walking towards the wood.

After a while, the Wolfshead Tree loomed up before him and he stared at its knots and mossy splits and couldn't see any signs of it falling down or being anything but solid. His eyes fell on a large hole, halfway up the tree.

'It's still there' came a small voice from behind him. Joe had caught him up and he and Cait had followed Max's gaze.

'What is it?' Cait asked

Max looked again at the object poking out of the knot hole. He couldn't remember seeing it before, surely he would have seen it if it had been there? He had seen this tree so many times he thought he knew everything about it. He made a decision.

'I'm climbing up' he said.

'It's … a long way' gulped Cait even though she really wanted to see what the object was.

Max put his foot in one of the holes, then found another and another and to his amazement he realised it was almost like a ladder leading him to the prize. On reaching the last branch before the hole, he hooked his arm round it and stretched up; making a grab for the thing that was hanging out. He pulled it down in front of him in disgust.

'It's only an old cow's horn' he shouted.

'Bring it down, let's have a look' shouted another voice and Max looked down to see Jake and Ethan had just arrived.

When he reached the ground, they all had a good look at it.

'It's not an ordinary cow's horn…'

'It's a bull's horn isn't it – it's huge!' interrupted Jake.

Max gave him a withering look and went on, 'Because it's got a leather strap attached to it and a piece of metal at each end.'

'It looks just like my trumpet mouthpiece' said Cait, 'Blow it Max, see if it makes a noise.'

'Yuk, it's filthy!'

'Wipe it with my hanky' suggested Joe, bringing out a dirty mud-covered handkerchief from his pocket.

'Er, no thanks' said Max and quickly wiping the pointed end on his sleeve, he gave the horn an almighty blow.

Woooo-ooo-ooo!

The sound was unexpectedly loud and echoed around the wood, bouncing off the trees. Everyone stood still for a moment expecting something to happen and were quite disappointed when it didn't.

'Try it again. That was weird' shivered Cait.

Everyone was staring at Max, waiting for the next blast so he duly obliged.

WOOOO-OOO-OOO!

The sound was even louder this time.

Suddenly they saw a movement in the shelter of the tree trunk. Then there was a voice, so unexpected that Max dropped the horn and everyone else jumped.

'Alright, alright' said the voice, 'I heard you the first time. Now who wants my help and what for? And it had better be good because you woke me from a very nice dream. By the way, what year is it?

CHAPTER 2

Everyone took an involuntary step back as the owner of the voice unfurled himself from inside the hole at the bottom of the tree. He was a tall, dark-haired, good-looking young man dressed in a peculiar green tunic and what could only be described as brown leggings – leather by the look of them – with soft crumply leather boots on his feet. The man's head was partially covered by a hood which was attached to his tunic. On a leather belt round his tunic he carried a quiver full of arrows and he held a longbow in his hands. Joe's eyes nearly popped out of his head.

'Blimey! It's Robin Hood!' he squealed.

'Don't be silly' growled Cait out of the side of her mouth whilst grabbing Joe's hand so they could make a quick getaway if needed. The others were all rooted to the spot.

'It is' insisted Joe, 'I've seen him in my storybook.'

A friendly smile appeared on the stranger's face and a snorting noise, which Max realised was a laugh, escaped from his mouth as he crouched down to Joe's level.

You're right in a way little man' he laughed 'That's what everyone has always called me because of this hood I pull over my head to disguise myself but my original name was Robin Wood of Buckton, son of Robin Smelleather of Sherburn'

Max looked at Ethan who looked at Jake, who looked at the floor. They tried for a few seconds not to laugh but in the end Ethan started giggling which set the others off too, as nervous as they felt. Max didn't join in though as he wasn't sure it was quite the right thing to do.

'Smelleather?' Ethan laughed

'Yes, Smelleather.' Robin said haughtily, looking quite put out. The giggling didn't stop so he attempted a few words of explanation.

'My father made things out of leather and so I suppose, smelled of it, hence the name.'

'Did they call him smelly for short?' sniggered Ethan again, warming to the subject.

'They daren't – he would have killed them if they'd tried'

This shut Ethan and the rest of them up immediately.

'In Old England, our names came from what we did or what we looked like. Mine was Robin Wood as we lived in Buckton which was then a village in the middle of the woods, which were then much bigger than this. It changed later to Robin Hood from the hood I use to disguise myself when evading capture'

'What were you getting captured for? asked Cait with a worried expression on her face.

'Oh, various things but don't worry, I'm generally on the side of right and not wrong. Unless someone' he looked at Ethan pointedly, 'starts to get on my nerves' Robin had started to sulk and slowly turned away from them.

'I'm sure we don't mean to be rude sir' he ventured to the now miserable looking figure of

Robin who was staring at the ground with a frown. Max thought he'd change the subject, 'It's just that you don't hear names like that now' he remembered Robin's question when they first saw him, 'in 2022.'

'2022?' Robin stopped in the middle of folding his arms and sulking and instead jumped onto a fallen tree trunk that all the friends used as a seat.

'Od's boddikins! It's been a rare sleep since the last call. It's not often I get the luxury of more than a quick nap of a hundred years.'

'A hundred years is a quick nap?' said Max and looked at the others who had stopped smirking and were now looking worried again.

'Perhaps,' muttered Robin, lost in thought, 'it's just that people don't need me as much as they did.' He lowered his head.

He looked so unbearably sad that even Cait felt sorry for him.

'What sort of thing do people need you for?' she asked to break the silence.

'Well,' he said brightening up slightly, 'the sort of thing that YOU need me for I should imagine.' He swept his arm across indicating the group of them.

'W-we need you?' stammered Jake

'Yes. You called me didn't you? On the horn?'

'Well yes,' said Max, looking down at the hunting horn he had picked up again. 'I blew it but we didn't know what it was for'

'The hunting horn only appears when someone desperately needs my help. You must have asked for help...didn't you?' said Robin looking almost as puzzled as the rest of them.

'No, I...' started Max then suddenly he remembered the day before when he was angry over Cheetingham's plans. 'We need help' he had said and that was when Joe first saw the horn in the tree.

'I suppose I did ask for your help really but how can you help us?

'I can shoot your enemies at 100 yards, straight through the heart' Robin said pleasantly as Cait and Max looked at each other in horror.

'I don't think that would be a good idea. You can get put in prison for things like that now' warned Max.

'You got put in prison for it then' remembered Robin sadly and then brightened up 'but I always managed to get out. I suppose there are other ways though if you insist.'

'Have you got any magic powers?' said Joe, his eyes wide with wonder.

'Don't be silly, Robin Hood can shoot a good arrow but he's not magic.' smiled Jake.

Robin stared fixedly into Jake's eyes, which made Jake feel like a rabbit caught in headlights.

'Excuse me,' said Robin folding his arms menacingly, 'From what I've told you, you'll be able to work out that I am a good deal older than I look – about a thousand years older by my calculations - and I have just appeared out of the tree after a sleep of over a hundred years – and you still don't think I'm magic? What do I have to do to convince you young sir? Produce something out of thin air?'

Robin had growled the last question and none of them wanted to ask him to prove anything but

Cait couldn't stand the long silence while he waited for them to reply.

'Well...' she started

Shooom! There was a peculiar rushing noise all around them and suddenly, there on Robin's hand sat a particularly large and ugly-looking crow. The crow looked from one to the other of them with beady yellow crow-eyes, almost daring them to speak. Robin looked very satisfied with himself and having successfully put them in their place; he sighed and stretched out on the ground, leaning against the tree.

'So, again, how can I help?'

'They're going to...' began Ethan and Jake together.

'Hang on, hang on – you, the blond one with the hair in his face – you tell me.'

Max flicked the hair back out of his eyes but was secretly pleased to have been chosen.

'They're going to divert the stream to the fishing lake at the manor, cut down the trees and build...something. We heard them talking about their plans yesterday. Whatever it is, we don't want it. These woods have been here for...'

'More than a thousand years' finished Robin, 'yes I know, I've been in them remember? Who is doing this?'

'Cheetingham'

Robin laughed sourly, 'He certainly is cheeting'em. Cheating'em out of a good place for children to play. Not to mention the birds and squirrels and insects that live in the trees or the fish in the stream or other wildlife that finds a haven in these woods' Robin shook his head sadly, 'Of course I'll help.'

'Yayy!' they all shouted, jumping up and down.

'Do you have a plan?' Robin enquired and they all stopped jumping.

'Isn't that your department?' asked Cait 'I mean, haven't you done anything like this before? You should be the leader and we can help you.'

'Ah, a bossy female! You remind me of a fair maiden I knew many years ago.'

'Maid Marian?' ventured Cait?

'Good Heavens, no idea, one of many I'm afraid.'

Cait scowled at him.

'Okay' said Robin suddenly, 'I think I can feel a plan coming on. Try and get some information – why, where, who, how and what – and meet me here tomorrow at midday.'

'Is that because it's a magic time?' asked Joe.

'No, it's because I want a lay-in. Still not properly awake yet. Off you go then.' Robin shooed them away.

The others looked at each other and began wandering reluctantly in the direction of home. When they had gone a short distance and could no longer see Robin, Max turned to the others.

'Strange bloke' he said

'Bloke? He doesn't look that much older than us' said Cait.

'Not normal is it though, coming out of a tree like Rip Van Winkle with tights on? Still, do you really think he can help us?' Max frowned.

'I think' said Cait,' that as we're all under the age of twelve, our parents never take us seriously and nobody else will listen to us – that you're looking at your best bet so far.'

They all nodded doubtfully to each other then parted on their different ways: Ethan and Jake to where they lived on the same road, on the outskirts of Buckton and Max, Cait and Joe to their farmhouse nearby. They were all lost in thought and very confused.

Chapter 3

All was quiet at Hartshead Farm where Max lived. It was well past midnight and everyone was in bed.

Ping!

Max stirred slightly in his sleep.

Ping! Ping!

Now awake, he looked over to the window where the sound was coming from. The moonlight shone a beam through a gap in the curtains. Rubbing his eyes he stumbled over and peered through the glass. He rubbed his eyes again, this time to make sure he was really seeing Robin Hood standing in the middle of his garden throwing stones at this window. A stone pinged again so he opened the window.

'What do you want?' he said in a loud whisper so as not to wake his parents.

'I'm starving.

'What?'

'I'm starving!'

'Can't it wait till tomorrow; it's the middle of the night?'

'Look, young fellow-me-lad, if you'd had to wait many, many years for your next decent meal, you'd be starving too. I keep getting woken up by my stomach. It's rumbling like one of those big things with wheels.'

'Car…lorry?'

'No, no.'

'Train?'

'That could be the one! Now be a good lad and bring me some food. Ale would be an excellent idea too.'

Max sighed and went across the landing, then deciding he didn't know what thousand-year-old people ate, he went to wake Cait. Joe appeared at his bedroom door.

'What do magic people eat?' he asked as Cait threw on her dressing gown and they made for the kitchen.

'Same as us, like it or lump it.' growled Cait as she started to tear a chicken leg off the cooked chicken in the fridge.

'What's he saying?' Joe pointed at the back door window where Robin was making gnawing motions on an imaginary piece of meat.

'Oh God' sighed Cait and took the whole chicken out.

'You'll be for it tomorrow when mum and dad see it's missing' scolded Max.

'No you will, you'll have to think of something. Say you were sleepwalking and ate the chicken or something. You're the one who called him to help us after all.'

Max shook his head, 'I think he's going to be more trouble than help.'

They quietly opened the back door and two hands shot out and grabbed the chicken which he stuffed inside his tunic. It was joined by a bottle of beer Max had taken from the fridge. He then grabbed the lone chicken leg that Cait held separately.

'Mm mmmf grmmf,' he said, his mouth full of chicken.

'What?' chorused Max and Cait.

'Any fruit?' he managed to say between mouthfuls.

Max went in and grabbed three apples from the fruit bowl. He threw them one at a time to Robin who caught them perfectly.

'Many thanks. I'll see you tomorrow. Time you were in bed isn't it?' he laughed, winking at them.

The last thing they saw before they closed the door was Robin juggling three apples as he walked down the path.

Back at the Wolfshead Tree, Robin once again settled in the hole at the bottom of the tree but if you had passed by, you would have seen nothing there except perhaps for the large, strange-looking crow keeping guard on a low branch. Before he finally went to sleep, Robin thought about the day's events.

'Cheetingham?' he mumbled to himself, stifling a yawn, 'Now where have I heard that name before?'

CHAPTER 4

The day dawned bright and early and Max's parents found lots for him to do before he could think about getting away to Robbers' Wood. His mother kept up a running commentary.

'Tidy that bedroom out, it's disgusting. Do you think those plates are going to clean themselves? I don't know how you can eat so much breakfast after eating a full chicken to yourself. Take those library books back or you'll have a fine.'

At last, thought Max, a chance to get away. He grabbed the books off the sideboard and whispered to Cait that he would meet them at the Wolfshead Tree before rushing down into Buckton. He returned the books to the library, stopping briefly to read a notice pinned on the noticeboard outside.

After calling for Ethan and Jake, they all rushed up the hill, over the field and into the wood. Breathless, they reached the tree just after Cait and Joe who were just sitting down.

'He's not here.' said Cait.

'What time is it?' asked Ethan while Max looked at this watch.

'Five past twelve. He should be here. He wouldn't let us down. Would he?'

Suddenly a branchful of leaves in the tree shivered and Robin jumped down from it, making them all jump.

'The art of camouflage and one you will have to master if you're going to be any use to me.' he said superciliously.

'Oh blimey, it's the SAS!' whispered Max.

'Gather round my friends and listen to the plan' said Robin and they dutifully sat around him as he stood importantly in the middle of them.

'Now, as I understand it, you don't want Cheetingham shot by an arrow…or sliced through by a sword?' he added hopefully. They shook their heads.

'Alright' he said sadly, 'in that case, it will take longer than a day so we're looking at maybe two days.'

'What do you think you can do in two days that doesn't involve killing people' sneered Cait.

'First' continued Robin, 'I need to know the names of the people involved and where they live.'

'It's Cheetingham, that's all we know and he lives in the huge house at the bottom of the hill right over there.' Ethan pointed somewhere to the left of Buckton.

'Well in that case…' began Robin

'Technically you're right' broke in Max, 'but I've just read the notice at Buckton library and Cheetingham is the name of the company, after Cheetingham Manor where he lives, the one Ethan pointed out to you' he said looking at Robin 'He's building a private Leisure Club and Spa, whatever that is. His actual name is Albert Gisburn'

Robin turned white, then red, then spluttered until the others thought he was going to choke, and then eventually managed to spit out

'Gisburn? GISBURN?! It can't be, I killed him years ago. No, of course it can't have been him and his name wasn't Albert but it must be the same family, they infested this area and it seems they still do. They are trouble! GISBURN!' he shouted incredulously.

After a short silence where Robin seemed lost in thought, Joe ventured a question, while cuddling up safely to Max's shoulder,

'Wh-ho is he?' He daren't even say the name that seemed to make Robin very angry indeed.

'Who is he?' roared Robin, 'Only my most deadly foe, my worst enemy in the world whether he's a descendant or not. They have been evil throughout the ages. There has never been a good Gisburn'

He looked at the friends sat on the floor, who were almost wishing the old, jokey Robin would come back.

'Now I'm here for as long as it takes. I won't rest until we beat him. This. Is. Personal.' he growled and the scowl on his face prevented the others from doing anything but nodding silently

Meanwhile, at Cheetingham Manor, Albert Gisburn was chuckling at a letter he had received from the council saying -

'We are not of a mind to grant you permission to build a Leisure Club on your land known as Robbers' Wood, as it is common land and used by the community of this town to exercise their ancient rights. However, as you say, we do not seem to be able to produce a document which proves the wood is common land and which would prove that the common law is not just – in your words – an ancient myth. Your plans would appear to be using the outer trees to screen the new complcx from the road and town and would only need to fell an acre of the trees and re-route the stream which runs through it. Unfortunately, you have the right to cut down the trees if it is your own land. Unless we can produce the document which gives Buckton common rights over the woods in one month from now, it will have to be assumed that your plans can go ahead after you meet with the committee again. However, we would ask you to take all the deeds to your land in to our legal department as soon as possible so they may check all the details. Therefore, we will postpone any decision until a month from now.'

'Ha!' snorted Gisburn, 'and you thought you could beat me. This was my ancestor's land and

33

you'll never find any document about common rights in the wood.' At this, he smiled deviously. 'No, you won't find it; no matter how hard you try because people have been searching for centuries, including my family just so we could destroy the document. Right, my solicitor will take the deeds to the council tomorrow, to prove my absolute ownership of the woods.'

Today though, he had to go and hire some more contractors. The local ones had refused to cut down the trees. Some superstitious nonsense about 'disturbing the wood spirits'. Idiots, he thought to himself, carefully folding the letter and putting that and the deeds in his desk drawer.

As soon as he had left the room, two hands appeared on the outside of the window and their owner peered into the office.

'Hmm, interesting. Well, you heard him. He needs to take those deeds in before a decision can be made – so we need those deeds. At least it will delay them a while.

'Good idea' agreed Max.

'Yes, well, I've had the idea so it's only right that you should get the deeds.'

'What? Me? How?' replied Max in a panic.

Robin sighed and pointed to the slightly open window.

'Like this' he said and pulled at the window which stuck after a couple of seconds but still left enough room for Max to squeeze through.

His heart was hammering as he let himself down onto the floor and he tiptoed across to the desk. Opening the drawer, he looked at Robin who had been joined by Cait and Joe. Robin nodded his encouragement and Max grabbed the deeds, re-closing the drawer after him. He was just on his way back with a big grin on his face when he heard a noise outside the door. Joe put his hands over his eyes and ducked; while Cait pointed down under the desk then joined Joe. Robin was nowhere to be seen.

Max dropped down to the floor and crawled under the desk just before Gisburn walked back into the room, reading from some other papers. He made his way slowly over to the desk, still reading.

Oh no, thought Max, he's coming to put them in the desk. I'm done for! He peeped out from the other side to see if he could make a run for it, just in time to see Gisburn shiver and go over to the window looking quite puzzled as to how it was open so far. He shut it and turned towards the desk again as Cait and Joe's horrified faces popped up at the window. Max's mouth formed the silent words 'I'm dead'.

Suddenly, the sound of a hunting horn echoed loudly nearby. It sounded like it was in the house itself. Gisburn whirled round in shock then slowly made for the door before he jumped two inches into the air. There it was again, even louder. There was no mistaking it this time, it sounded just like the horn they used in the Cheetingham Hunt which was hung in the Great Hall next door. He opened the door cautiously and peered round it to the wall next to the staircase. The horn was gone! Who was playing games with him? They would soon learn that you didn't make a fool out of Albert Gisburn.

Gisburn moved across the hall towards an open door at the other side leading to the drawing room. A noise came from inside the room. He grabbed a large vase from a hall stand outside the door and shuffled into the room.

Meanwhile, Max had crawled back towards the window where Cait had pulled it up again. He managed to squeeze through and drop into the garden. At the same time, Robin jumped down from the drawing room window, the hunting horn still in his hand and a sheet of paper held between his teeth. He motioned for them to meet him outside the front door, which he opened quietly .

'Go over to Ethan and Jake in the bushes and get ready to run when I do.' Robin whispered.

They did so and watched in trepidation as Robin pulled the bow from his back and an arrow from the quiver. Cait closed her eyes and crossed her fingers.

Back in the drawing room, Gisburn had finished searching behind settees and cupboards, finally sitting down in his chair with a frown. Suddenly, the horn sounded loudly, making him drop the vase he still carried which shattered into hundreds of pieces. He rushed into the hall and saw the main entrance door was wide open. He went towards it then drew back in horror as an arrow shot past his face just missing his rather large nose. It embedded itself in the wall in the exact place the hunting horn had been hanging.

'What the…!' he spluttered before he realised there was something wrapped round the arrow. He ran across and grabbed the paper which he saw was a piece of his own personal writing paper with the Gisburn crest on it, which he kept in the drawing room. He read the hastily scribbled message with alarm.

HANDS OFF ROBBERS' WOOD

THIS IS WAR, GISBURN!

It was signed simply 'Hood'.

'Charters. CHARTERS!' he shouted to his butler, 'did you anyone run out of here with the hunting horn?'

Charters, who personally thought his master was losing his marbles, looked at him gravely, sighed and went back to the kitchen.

Gisburn shook his head in a daze. Who on earth was Hood? He had expected opposition from the town but that arrow could have killed him. Unless it was someone who was very, very good with a bow and knew exactly what he was doing. Something, somewhere deep in his memory stirred and he frowned again. Going to the door, he cautiously looked out but there was no-one on the drive or in the garden. Whoever it was had gone - and good riddance. He slammed the door shut.

Robin and the others were already halfway up the hill, keeping to the other side of the hedge and had soon entered the wood. Here they collapsed on the floor laughing. Max waved the deeds.

'This should stop him, for a while at least.'

'That man's face looked funny when you nearly shot his nose off Robin.' giggled Joe, thinking of how they had watched from the bushes.

'And you've still got his hunting horn' said Cait, pointing to the prize hanging round Robin's neck. It was much more ornate than the other horn as it had silver on the mouthpiece and what looked like a gold band round it.

'*His* hunting horn be blowed, if you'll pardon the pun. It's *my* hunting horn! One of his forefathers stole it from me long ago and he's not getting it back again now.' grinned Robin.

With that he blew an almighty note on the horn. The sound travelled over the fields and into the grounds of Cheetingham Manor to be heard again by Albert Gisburn, who froze on the spot. This time, as his family's history entered his mind, he thought he knew who was blowing the horn – and he didn't like it one bit.

CHAPTER 5

'Who told you this Ethan?' asked Max

'It was a friend of my cousin Alf's called Bryn whose father knows the brother of one of the builders who's going to work on the Robbers' Wood site.' Ethan took a deep breath to give the others time to digest this information. Instead they merely looked puzzled.

'Anyway, what it means is, the copy of the deeds you stole was just that – a copy. Gisburn's solicitor has got the original. It also means that Gisburn can go ahead in a couple of weeks' time as the council can't prove that the wood is common land with rights for the townspeople. They're supposed to be looking for the document but Bryn's father's friend's...' Ethan stopped as they all groaned.

'Yes, we get the general idea.'

'What's even worse is that…this bloke said it's not going to be a leisure club; it's going to be an undercover gambling den for all Gisburn's city friends. It's private so nobody from Buckton can use it and what's left of the wood will have 'Trespassers Prosecuted' all round it.' Ethan finished his announcement and looked at Max.

'It's looking bad. We need Robin. Where is he?' said Max peering into the hole at the bottom of the Wolfshead Tree.

The others shrugged their shoulders or shook their heads and a mood of melancholy hung in the air. Suddenly there was a noise from over near a fallen tree as Robin crunched over the dead bark with his boots.

'Oh dear,' he said with an amused glance at the group in front of him, 'Has someone taken your toys away?'

'We've had some bad news' growled Max.

'And where've you been anyway? whined Cait.

'Practising the bow. It should be done every day until you're perfect. Like me.' He added raising an eyebrow but even though they knew he was just trying to get a reaction from them, they still sat there staring at the ground. There was a loud rustle from the branches above their heads and a rather large crow fell upside down and unmoving at their feet.

'Yuk!' said Jake as he sprung backwards.

'You awful bully' Cait shouted at Robin, 'look what you've done!'

'Wh… ? Me? stuttered Robin open-mouthed, 'Wh…what…? Robin held his hands towards the others in a mute plea.

'Don't you look innocent' scowled Cait who like animals and birds better than humans, 'you said you've been shooting arrows and you've Killed This Crow!'

'I've what?' Robin looked surprised, 'I've done nothing of the sort!'

'Look at the poor thing.' pointed Cait and everyone looked down at the crow, laid on its back with its feet in the air. As they watched, one of the legs gave a feeble twitch and Cait threw herself down next to it.

'Come on someone, help me wrap it up and we'll take it to the vets. It's still alive.'

'Of course it's alive.' said Robin scornfully, 'Do you see an arrow stuck in it? Do you see blood?'

They all moved closer as Cait bent to examine the bird.

'Oh for heaven's sake Charlie, stop acting the fool, you're scaring the children. Behave yourself!'

After another twitch of the leg for good measure, the crow opened his yellow crow-eyes, looked beadily round and jumped swiftly up, shaking his feathers. Charlie then flew onto Robin's shoulder accompanied by a gasp from the incredulous audience.

'Do you know the crow?' asked Joe in astonishment.

'Oh poetry! I love poetry' grinned Robin. 'Yes, I do – Know the Crow.' He turned to gaze into two menacing little eyes and sighed. 'How's this for poetry?'

This bird is dumb

And a pain in the bum.

If it tries to peck,

I'll wring its scraggy neck.

The bird slowly turned its eyes away from Robin and faced the other direction sulkily as the others stared in disbelief.

'Very good' said Joe after a few seconds.

'What?' asked Max.

'The poem. Very good.'

Max put his head in his hand and tried to banish all thoughts of the last few bizarre minutes from his head.

'Can we just get on please and find some way to stop Gisburn getting rid of this?' and he gestured all around him at the woodland.

Robin sat on the ground and smirked.

'I have a plan.' he whispered, taking Charlie Crow off his shoulder and placing him on the ground beside him where he continued to sulk.

'Congratulations Einstein' said Cait who was still feeling annoyed that she had been tricked by a crow she had felt sorry for. 'What is it?'

'No please, let's hear your plan first' replied Robin sarcastically.

'I er, I haven't got one yet' mumbled Cait.

'As I thought, so listen to me now. It appears they have measured out the site of the buildings with stakes and twine?'

'Over half the wood is covered with them and they haven't even got permission yet.' moaned Max.

'So first we take it all down, you lot can do that and it will slow them up as they'll have to survey and measure it all up again. Any obstacle we can put in their way, however small, is going to seriously annoy Gisburn too, which is a plus for me. I have another way to delay things for a while longer though. Come closer…'

*

Nearly an hour later, with the help of Evie and Eira who had come to Max's house and had run to find everyone - all the stakes and twine had been pulled up and dragged to different parts of the wood, they followed Robin down to the far end of what was called Brewer's Lake. It really only looked like a large pond and the children of Buckton had gathered frogspawn there for years. At this end, the water narrowed into a stream which then split into two. The first widened into a fast-flowing stream that ran down the field and

45

along the valley in front of Cheetingham Manor and the large lake. The other side had long since dwindled into just a trickle, a small brook meandering through the woods and then down below Max's house. He couldn't remember there ever being much water in apart from when there was heavy rain and then it gushed along - a dirty brown colour – only to disappear into a muddy mess a few days later.

'I still don't think it's going to work.' ventured Max quietly, thinking of the plan Robin had revealed to them earlier.

'Oh ye of little faith.' chastised Robin and started picking up the biggest stones he could find. Although they couldn't match the boulder-size rocks that Robin was finding, they all kept busy putting their stones where Robin had placed his. After a while they had built a substantial dam across the main stream and the water was bubbling and swirling in front of the rocks, not knowing which way to go.

'Don't think that's going to flood the ground, do you?' said Cait shaking her head.

'We haven't finished yet' grunted Robin, 'start digging.'

'With what?' said Jake.

'Oh I forgot to put my spade in my pocket when I came out.' said Ethan with a grin.

Robin looked hurt.

'Improvise' he growled, pointing at some large jagged stones nearby.

'It'll take forever' Max sniffed, 'and it'll only take me five minutes to go home and fetch a couple of my dad's shovels.'

'Good idea' said Robin scowling 'and when the ground floods tomorrow, you can explain to your parents or anyone else who sees you that you only wanted the spades to make mud pies with.'

Max looked crestfallen.

'I could hide them…somehow' he grumbled.

No time. Come on – just get on with it' ordered Robin.

They dug a narrow trench just in front of their dam which diverted the water into the almost dry stream which ran by the side of Cheetingham's intended building site.

'It's just like building sandcastles with moats' said Joe

'Same principle I suppose, diverting the water from the sea to your moat' pondered Jake.

'Exactly, you're getting the idea now.' nodded Robin.

Cait looked at Evie and Eira who were only two years older than Joe. They had been a little scared of Robin when they first saw him and were shocked into silence – which was very unusual for them – but now they were helping the others as much as they could. They were covered from head to foot in mud and water. Their long curly hair – one red, the other blonde - was matted with mud and sticking out at all angles.

'Your mum is going to kill us' Cait pulled a face.

'More likely *your* Mum will kill us if we walk on her kitchen floor like this!' laughed Evie.

'She'll turn the hosepipe on us' said Eira.

Max laughed at them but then looked down at the dam and shook his head.

'It's going to need a torrential downpour to make any difference, so it's not likely. There's a drought and a hosepipe ban. We haven't had rain for ages and there's none forecast either. Dad's always grumbling about the state of his garden.'

Robin stared gravely at Max for a full twenty seconds before throwing down the sharp stone he was holding. He turned round and walked off swiftly into the woods. From the expression on his face they knew not to follow him. Charlie Crow, who had accompanied them, was now perched on a branch eyeing them solemnly. He seemed to give an exaggerated sigh and flew off after Robin.

'Now you've done it.' warned Cait.

'Well, he's just not being very realistic – is he?'

'…and you've managed to offend the crow too' continued Cait.

'Stuff the crow!' said Max, with feeling.

They all started off home in an uncomfortable silence but by the time they had reached the edge of the wood, the first raindrops had started to fall.

CHAPTER 6

'You can't leave Jake out; he's got to come too' pleaded Max.

It was later the same day and Ethan was stood there with Max and the others.

'It's Ethan's parents who have to leave him while they travel up to Edinburgh so that's why he has to stay tonight. It's not a sleepover Max!' scolded his mum. 'Even though your cousins are here, it's because your aunt and uncle are away too. It will be like circus if you're all staying'

'But that's just it Mum, it's just one more. Jake will feel left out if everyone else is here won't he? We're always together, you know we are.'

Max's mum and sighed and turned to her husband George.

'It's a filthy night and I don't know whether Jake's father would want him coming out on a night like this with a torrential rainstorm out there!'

Max, Cait, Joe and Ethan all turned and grinned at each other.

'That's why we want him to come!' they laughed.

'You are strange children' said George Cooper, looking at four eager faces. He folded his arms. 'Alright, I'll phone Jake's dad.'

The last words were drowned out by excited shouts coming from the children.

'BUT' he shouted, 'to continue… you must be asleep at a decent time, no noise – and no eating us out of house and home like you did last time.'

'We promise!' they all chorused.

'And that's if Jake is even allowed to come' finished Mr.Cooper.

Half an hour later a car pulled up at the garden gate and Jake made a dash for it, hood pulled up and trainers splashing down the path. After a quick wave and a few hardly audible exchanges between their fathers, Max led Jake, barefoot and coatless now, into the large attic room which they used as a den and where they were all camped out now. The Terrible Twins were dancing round pretending to be afraid of the thunder when a really bad bang from the sky made them scuttle for the corner and pull a blanket over their heads. They were still giggling though.

'Joe' shouted Evie and Joe crawled under for a minute before deciding he was brave and crawled out again.

'Omigod! Look at it.' laughed Ethan as they went over to the big dormer window to see the rain, the torrential rain that seemed like it would never stop, driving down on the land around – and most importantly – on Robbers' Wood.

At the very moment they had all managed to find a place to press their noses against on the window panes, the sky lit up, as a sheet of lightning spread across the horizon showing the outline of Buckton town silhouetted against it. They all sprang back in surprise.

'Whoa, that was a good one.' said Max with feeling.

They were just moving their heads towards the window again when a booming crack of thunder invaded their ears and shook the house to its foundations. They looked around at each other, clearly shocked. They were crouching on the floor as though they'd been shot.

'I don't like it.' whimpered Joe wanting to run back to the blanket which Eira was now holding open for him.

'It's okay, it's only, erm, something to do with air pressure, I think?' said Cait, putting her arm round Joe but really feeling anything but brave herself.

'Do you really think it's Robin who made this storm?' asked Joe in a quiet voice, 'because if it is, he must be very angry.'

The same thought had occurred to Max but he smiled at Joe.

'Robin? No, it's nature, that's all.'

'But it's like you said, there has been a drought and no rain forecast for weeks – and now look at it.' said Jake, wide-eyed.

'And he did say he was magic.' whispered Joe.

The lightning stopped the conversation as it lit up the room again. Then with a few feeble flickers, the two lamps went out just as the second clap of thunder echoed around the walls, making them dive for the floor.

Although the lamps flickered back on after a moment or two, the storm went on for some time . There were only whispered words and unbelieving glances betraying their surprise at the severity of the storm and the worry that it could actually have been caused by Robin. The jovial, carefree Robin was now far from their minds as he now appeared in their minds as some sort of thunder-god and they wondered what they had really got themselves into.

Eventually, the storm died away but the rain kept on falling relentlessly, the drops drumming like rapid gunfire on the flat top of the dormer window and making the view from the window impossible to see. Max brought out the chocolate, coke and bags of crisps that he had smuggled from the kitchen earlier and they all sat in a circle in reverential silence, devouring the illegal goodies. Cait looked annoyed at the silence after a while, keeping quiet had never been her strong point but she felt like interrupting the silence would somehow be wrong. Instead she restlessly pulled herself up and tried to peer out of the window. She stepped back in surprise then tried to clear some of the rain off the window to get a better look.

'The rain is on the outside' said Max sarcastically, 'I think you'll find it doesn't clear.'

Cait was too excited to be annoyed. She peered again at the figure leaning against the large beech tree in the garden.

'Robin's here, I think?' she trailed off uncertainly. There was a mad rush for the window and Max lifted the latch up. He opened the window and unleashed a torrent of water which wet their faces.

'Eurgh! It's all wet,' moaned Joe.

'Funny that, wet rain?' grinned Ethan as he scrabbled to catch a glimpse of Robin.

'I wonder what he wants?' asked Joe, his eyes just managing to peer over the sill.

'I don't know, he's probably gloating because he was right and I was wrong.' frowned Max but waved a rain-soaked arm through the window at Robin.

There was no need to get his attention though as Robin was staring straight up at the window without moving. As they watched he turned slowly, seemingly oblivious to the rain and walked off in the direction of the wood. They watched silently then Max shut the window as Cait passed a towel round. They glanced ominously at each other as they dried themselves before Jake broke the silence.

'Seems like he's in a bit of a mood with us eh? Again.'

Another moment passed before Cait spoke.

'No wonder with Max going on to him all the time about not believing him.'

'Hah! You can talk, nagging him about shooting crows when he hadn't.'

Cait put the blankets over the twins, who had fallen asleep on the floor next to each other, despite all the excitement. .

Silence descended again, broken a minute later by Max speaking the words they had all been thinking since the rain had begun.

'I think maybe we all ought to apologise to him for doubting him. After all, he pulled off the impossible and if we're going to save Robbers' Wood, he's our only hope.'

CHAPTER 7

The next morning they awoke to a different world. The rain had stopped, the sun was out and there was a fresh scent in the air. Max woke everyone and they all dragged on their clothes, eager to see if any damage had been done to Cheetingham's building site. With an increasing rumble which sounded like the roof was caving in, all seven of them ran down the stairs and towards the front door.

'Not so fast! Where do you think you're going?' asked Max's mum, leaning against the kitchen doorway.

'We've got to go out.' replied Joe.

'*Got* to have we? Without breakfast?' she smiled.

Max, Cait and Joe looked at each other.

'You see Mrs. Cooper, it's quite urgent...' began Jake.

'It's bacon, sausages, hash browns and beans' went on Mrs.Cooper, 'and it's ready now.'

Ethan and Jake looked at each other as well and then back at Max's mum.

'and fried bread.' she finished and they all made a dash for the kitchen after realising how hungry the smell was making them. Max's dad and Bess and Ferg were already there.

'That rain's done the garden a power of good' he smiled.

Max tutted. As if that was important when the safety of Robbers' Wood was at stake.

After breakfast, Evie and Eira had to go back with their parents but made Max promise to tell them anything that happened.

Ten minutes and five full stomachs later they were on their way to the wood, squelching through the sodden grass and splashing mud halfway up their legs. They soon came across the part of the wood that had been earmarked for Gisburn's club and instead of an earth and moss floor, another lake had appeared. They moved closer, hardly able to believe their eyes. The whole floor of the proposed building was covered in deep, murky grey water.

'Hurray!'

'That's beaten 'em!'

'Try and build on that lot!'

'Yayyy!'

All their voices came in one jubilant rush.

They were still dancing round in glee when a truck made its way carefully through the trees and pulled up nearby. Two men in yellow work jackets walked down to the site and started shaking their heads, much to the children's delight.

A moment later a Range Rover appeared in the distance and a corpulent figure came huffing and puffing towards the men. Albert Gisburn of Cheetingham Ltd. looked like he was about to explode.

'What? How?!' he spluttered, 'didn't you idiots make any plans in case this sort of thing happened?' he squawked at the workmen.

'This sort of thing has never happened before.' stated the biggest one of the two, looking slightly miffed 'so how could we plan for it?'

Max and the others pretended to be talking amongst themselves but felt safe in the certainty that no-one could possibly blame them for this. How could five children have created a rainstorm of epic proportions that had flooded the work site and stopped any tree-felling or attempt at building until it had gone back to normal? They tried not to let the men see them grinning to each other.

Gisburn was hopping about, shaking his fists and generally going purple with rage, watched happily by the children, when Joe turned to face them, ready to do an impersonation of Gisburn. Instead, he pointed and nodded at something behind them. Turning suspiciously, they found Robin, leaning nonchalantly against a tree behind them. He had his arms crossed and was staring straight across at Gisburn with an amused expression on his face. Max looked from one to the other in concern.

'He'll see you.' he said finally.

'No he won't.' countered Robin.

'What – you're invisible?'

'He Can't See Me.' Robin repeated slowly as though talking to a particularly stupid classful of pupils.

At that moment, Gisburn looked straight across to where they were standing and as his eyes reached the spot where Robin stood, his face suddenly lost its colour and his mouth fell open.

'Are you sure?' whispered Cait urgently to Robin who raised his eyebrows in exasperation but otherwise didn't move.

'Yes', he said, even more firmly and they all turned back to look at Gisburn who was still fixed in the same position.

'Mr.Gisburn?' said the smaller of the two men. No answer.

'Mr.Gisburn? Sir?'

Gisburn suddenly became aware of the man's voice and tore his gaze away to meet the man's eyes.

'Everything okay sir?'

'Yes, yes – fine. I just, well – it felt like, for a minute…' he shook his head and thought better of trying to explain. A shadow. That's all it was. Yet an eerie and somehow familiar shadow. He shuddered and picked his way through the mud and water back to the Range Rover. The workmen were already on their way back. He needed to stop letting his mind wander and get on sorting this mess out.

Robin now visibly relaxed and slowly sank to the floor as though his energy had been drained. Max went and crouched down opposite to face him.

'I'd erm, I'd like to apologise to you.'

'Me too,' interrupted Cait.

'I think all of us agree on that' said Ethan and Jake nodded too.

'I don't want to apologise. I've always thought he was magic' piped up Joe. This made Robin smile and he put his head back against the tree, still looking tired. Max continued.

'You must admit, it's all a bit much to take in. I mean Robin Hood comes out of a tree after an extremely long sleep and floods Gisburn's site out?' He stopped, checking himself. 'But yes, I'm sorry for not believing in you – and like Ethan said, you're our only hope.'

Robin smiled at Max and slowly got to his feet.

'I'm going back to the Wolfshead Tree to have a rest – making myself invisible to my enemies drains the power from me. Come with me, I have something to say to you.

*

Even with Robin's power diminished, they struggled to keep up with his long strides and were out of breath by the time they reached the tree. Robin had adopted his familiar position with his back leaning against the Wolfshead Tree and the others gathered round him.

'I just want to talk to you about helping yourselves more' said Robin and then smiled at their worried expressions. 'When I use magic, I have to rest and this might be over a crucial time. I will have to leave you for short periods to recover. Therefore, you will have to take over at these times. I will tell you what to do if you need me to.'

'Will you be able to stay till it's done? 'asked Max frowning, 'you know, till the wood is safe?'

Robin put his knees up and rested his arms on them. He looked weary and his voice was lower than normal.

'I have never gone away without seeing anything through and I don't intend to this time either. At the end of the time though, I must return to where I came from.'

They all looked a little downcast at this, they were getting used to this strange person who had answered their call for help.

'You'll go back in there then?' said Joe pointing to the tree.

Robin managed a chuckle.

'Not exactly. That's just the entrance to my world. No questions!' he put his hand up as they all started asking about him at once.

'I will tell you this. I was once, when I was a very young man, the same age as I am now I suppose' he gave a surprised laugh, 'I was badly injured by an arrow shot from the Sheriff's men. Gisburn, the OTHER Gisburn – had told them where I was. I knew I was going to die so I crept into the hole in the trunk of this tree. I must have passed out because when I woke up, the soldiers hadn't found me and by some miracle, not only was I alive but I had no wounds. The tree had healed them. So, throughout the years, whenever someone in these woods desperately needs help, the tree calls on me to repay my debt and help them.'

Max turned to the others as they fell silent, stunned by his story. When they had come round a little, Max turned to face Robin again.

'We *do* really need your help and we'll be glad of it as long as you can give it - and we'll help as much as we can too. We can promise you' said Max seriously, knowing this meant as much to Robin as it did to them 'that we will *never* let Gisburn win.'

He found his fists were clenched and was glad when the others joined in and cheered. It was a big promise to make; he just hoped they could carry it out. Robin was smiling at him and he smiled back. In that moment he felt that Robin was far more clever than he let on, his eyes betrayed his intelligence.

'I know something you could do right now' said Robin. 'I happened to be in the vicinity of Cheetingham Manor first thing this morning. Gisburn was at the door talking to a man, so I hid round the corner and listened. Apparently the townspeople are having a meeting about the proposed club. They were told it was going to be a leisure club and had heard the rumours that the townspeople would be kept away from it. They were also led to believe that planning permission wouldn't be received. Now they are very angry that it may in fact be given. The meeting's this afternoon. Why don't you go and see what you can find out?'

They all looked worried and Cait voiced what they were thinking.

'It will be all adults; will they even let us in?'

'I'm sure you'll find some way. Pretend you're with some of the adults.' Robin gave a wry smile 'and I'm sure you'll find someone there who will be very helpful indeed'

Before they could ask what he meant, he disappeared into the tree. Really disappeared. There was no sign of him in the hole at the bottom; it was almost as though he had melted into the tree.

'He'll come back won't he?' whispered Joe, his bottom lip quivering.

Max straightened his shoulders and held his head high.

'Of course he will, you heard him. Come on, let's go into Buckton and see where this meeting is.'

CHAPTER 8

There on the noticeboard outside the Town Hall was a hastily-written notice in big black felt-tip letters.

MEETING IN ST. STEPHEN'S CHURCH HALL AT 2PM. COME AND VOICE YOUR OBJECTIONS TO CHEETINGHAM'S PLANS FOR ROBBERS' WOOD. LET'S STOP THIS TRAVESTY.

'What's a tar-ves-ty?' asked Joe, struggling with the word.

Cait sighed impatiently.

'It's a... well it's a...'

Ethan sniggered and the corners of Max's mouth twitched. Cait went bright pink and finally shouted,

'It's a thing that shouldn't be happening!'

'Well' said Max, 'that's something we all agree on.

He looked at his watch; there was half an hour to go yet until the start of the meeting. They sat on the low wall at the side of the Town Hall and waited until it was time to make their way to the Church Hall around the corner. Finally, they all went silently to the hall, not knowing exactly what they were doing there.

'Where do you think you're going?' said the man at the door sternly.

'In there' said Cait looking down her nose as she did when she was trying to be grown up, 'we've got as much right as anyone else.'

The man looked confused but then said,

'Any trouble from you and you're out. Understood?'

They all nodded and dashed in before he could change his mind. Even though there were seats nearer the front, they all sat at the back, conscious that they might be the only children there and not wanting to draw attention to themselves.

The hall soon filled up, in fact there were people standing at the sides and at the back. A man in a brown suit sat at the table on the stage. He had a bristly moustache which hung over his top lip and he looked around him nervously. He was soon joined by a youngish man with wavy blond hair and a wolfish smile showing very white teeth. He was wearing a grey suit with a bright red waistcoat and he eased himself into the second chair.

'Flash so and so' thought Max, his lip curling with dislike.

The third chair was taken up with the Vicar of St. Stephen's, the Reverend Rowley. He was a friend of Max's father and often came up to the cottage, leaving with a warm glow after demolishing a large supply of the Cooper's home-made wine. Ethan leant forward and smiled at the rest of them. They responded with a knowing look. They were all very fond of him but he cut a ridiculous figure sometimes, getting his words muddled up, putting his cassock on inside out and tripping over his own feet. It was as though his body was there but his mind was somewhere else. They all called him Rev Rowley with affection, although they had heard their parents call him

69

something less than flattering about his size and they all watched him as he lowered his tubby frame onto a frail-looking chair while they waited for the next disaster. It didn't come, the chair held fast. What did happen though was that he looked over the heads of the other people there and directly at the children, winking and smiling before looking away.

'You don't think…?' began Cait.

'That's what I was thinking.' Ethan replied.

'It can't be' whispered Max 'He can't help himself, let alone us!'

Nevertheless, the all looked at the Reverend with fresh eyes. Could he be the one who Robin said would be helpful to them?

The man in brown stood up and shouted 'Order!' Instantly the room became quiet.

'I am Herbert Archmount and I represent the council on this matter. On my right is William Scatlock, a partner in the local law firm of Scatlock, Bashall and Print. On my left as you probably know, is the Vicar of St. Stephen's, the Right Reverend Rowley.'

'Right Reverend Rowley' repeated Joe in a low whisper and began to giggle. Cait shushed him fiercely.

'This meeting has been called' Mr Archmount went on 'by Mr Cooper, Mr Barnes and Mr Birch, to address the building of the new club by Cheetingham's Ltd with a view to opposing it'

Five very surprised faces looked at the back views, unseen till now, of their fathers. Mr Barnes was Ethan's father and Jake's father Mr. Birch was there too, standing next to him. It seemed that their families were opposing the plans just like they were. Max allowed himself a proud smile. Somehow, he knew they would be doing the right thing and wished that he had confided in his parents.

'Mr.Scatlock, would you like to speak first? Mr Archmount sat down and the 'flash so and so' rose.

'I have here' he started, holding up a bundle of papers tied with black ribbon, 'a document brought in by Albert Gisburn of Cheetingham's, which is absolute proof – checked by a team of legal advisors – of Mr.Gisburn's ownership of the land around Cheetingham Manor. Therefore, this meeting is defeated before it can begin. Mr.Gisburn can do what he wants with his own land if he has the planning permission granted.'

The Church Hall erupted in a volley of sound as each person tried to make their own views heard. Max watched Scatlock as he sat back down and thought for a minute that he looked defeated but then the white sneering smile appeared and Max turned his nose up in disgust at his smug figure. Archmount once more called for 'Order' and the shouts turned into a disgruntled murmur as they once more took their seats.

'Yes Mr.Cooper' he said, pointing at Max's father who had remained standing and now started to speak, his voice sounding loud and clear across the Hall.

'I want to say that even if Gisburn does own Robbers' Wood, which we seriously doubt, surely the council can't give planning permission for such a monstrosity to be built in a rural area, for most of the trees to be chopped down and many animals and birds deprived of their natural habitat? Surely the views of the people of Buckton must be listened to? What about the freedom of the common land, the old Rights of Way? Are hundreds of years of history just going to be ignored?

There were shouts of agreement and encouragement all around them and the noise built up again. The Rev Rowley stood up and waved his arms around ineffectually for what seemed an age until everyone went quiet again. Rowley's face was pink with effort and he folded his fat arms on his substantial stomach.

'I know that feelings run high about this development and I'm afraid I must agree with you...'

The clamour started again as people nodded approvingly.

'But' Rowley said again, holding his arms up for silence, 'we must hear what these people have to say before we can draw any conclusions. Therefore I ask you for quiet so the Bayor of Muckton can speak. I-I mean the Mayor of Buckton of course.'

Rowley sat down looking very flustered but the angry murmurs had been temporarily replaced by chuckles, the loudest coming from Max and everyone. Joe however, looked surprised as Archmount stood up again. Where was his furry red coat and gold chain? He didn't look like a mayor.

Archmount stood up and looked at Max's father.

'I thank you for your question Mr Cooper and I have an answer for you. I am afraid the council has already approved planning permission dependent on two things. One was that Mr Gisburn proved absolute ownership of the land he wants to build on, as well as the surrounding acres. As this land is in the middle of the acreage and would not disturb anyone but Mr.Gisburn himself, we could then find no reason not to grant the permission. Unfortunately, as our eminent local solicitor, Mr Scatlock has confirmed, that according to the deeds, there is no doubt of the ownership. That, coupled with the employment it may bring to the area means, I'm afraid, that the club is likely to be built.'

At this, the whole crowd stood up together, roaring their disapproval. Mr.Cooper waved his arms to silence them all.

'I would just like to ask about the Common Land, the right we have as citizens of Buckton to use Robbers' Wood as our own.'

Archmount looked put out. You could have heard a pin drop as everyone held their breath for his reply.

'That is the second thing. Proof of the existence of the Common Land. We have been searching for such a document for a while now. We cannot find one. If no document is found by 9am on the seventeenth of the month, we will have to presume that it doesn't exist and just came down the years by word of mouth. The planning permission will then be granted.'

The men on the dais exchanged glances and rose from their seats. They started to walk down the aisle between the seats. The mood in the hall changed to one of silent resignation, as though that was it – there was nothing they could do about it. The footsteps of the three men echoed as they made their way towards the main door at the back. As they came towards him, Max looked around at all the stunned faces and then at the still-smiling face of Scatlock who was still clutching the deeds and something snapped inside him. All he could think was 'Is this it? Was it all for nothing?' Suddenly, to the surprise of his friends, Max stood on his chair.

'Wait!'

All eyes turned towards him in surprise.

'Are you giving up? Because they say they are going to go ahead – are you just going to let them? Robbers' Wood has belonged to us for longer than anyone can remember. Generations have played there, walked there, found peace away from the noise of the town. Why should we let them take that away from us without a fight? If we all join together and say 'No' we can make this work. Don't back down' he pleaded, 'Fight!'

For a moment no-one moved. The three men had stopped walking and were watching him. Overcome with embarrassment at what he had done, Max found himself looking straight into Scatlock's eyes and the wry amusement he found there made him jump down and run towards the door. His father caught him just before he reached it. He put his hands on his son's shoulders as Max looked fearfully up at him. Mr Cooper shook his head but then smiled gently.

'I'm proud of you son' he said quietly.

Haltingly, people began to clap and, as Max broke away and walked as slowly as he dare for the hall door, the whole place erupted in applause.

76

Cait ran up to Rev Rowley as people started to file out of the hall, talking animatedly.

'Rev Rowley, I mean Reverend – can we talk to you sometime? Soon? I think you may be able to help us.'

'Me? Well, if you think so. Perhaps tomorrow 10.30 a.m. in St. Stephens? I have to check the church is ready for a christening at 11.15.'

Meanwhile, Joe, standing just behind Cait, was watching the crowd disperse. Nearly everyone had gone out now. Ethan and Jake had run after Max to see if he was okay. Someone at the back caught his eye. He couldn't see his face as his hood was pulled over it and he kept his head down. Yet there was something in the effortless way he now walked out with long confident strides, his dark hair just showing at the edge of his hood. Robin was here!

CHAPTER 9

Max, Cait and Joe stared wide-eyed as they listened to their father's tales about Robbers' Wood after they had finished their breakfast. Mr Cooper had caught up with his son when he had run out of the Church Hall the day before and shook his hand like a grown-up. He had been amused but interested that they were all fighting for the same cause. The Cooper children's father was an historian who had written books about folk customs and traditions in the British Isles. He was telling them now about a legend concerning Robbers' Wood. The old story went that help always arrived when the wood was threatened. As if by magic he said. At this point it was all Max could do to not look at Cait and he could see Joe out of the corner of his eye bouncing about with excitement but Cait had given him a warning glance which stopped him mid-bounce. None of them were quite sure why they weren't confiding in their father, especially as he was telling them about the legend they knew to be true. It perhaps wasn't the time – not yet.

It was not only when the wood was threatened, their father was saying now but when the people of Buckton were too. There were many families still living here whose ancestors had lived here hundreds of years ago. The same surnames were recorded in the Domesday Book, court rolls and parish records that belonged to people living here today. The town had been threatened many times over the last thousand years but had always survived. Cait was digging Max in the ribs as their father talked about the legend and he knew what she was trying to say. Was it Robin who had helped before?

When Mr Cooper went out, Max ran off towards the wood followed closely by his brother and sister. He wanted to tell Robin that they had found the person who could help them and were meeting him that morning at the church. He felt ashamed of running off yesterday but he had always tried to keep out of the limelight and was shocked at what he had done and how much this matter meant to him. He could not have stood up like he did in front of all those people if he had not felt the fire burning in his heart.

On reaching the Wolfshead Tree they called for Robin but he was nowhere to be seen. They looked nearby and went down to the proposed building site in case he was there. Instead, they found a gang of workmen. No sooner had they arrived than a chainsaw started up.

'No!' cried Cait, the word escaping in a sob 'You can't!'

The men's faces turned towards the children and a big red-faced man took off his white helmet revealing a bald head and walked slowly towards them with narrowed eyes.

'What are you kids doing 'ere? I know you don't I? You were up here the other day.' He seemed to think for a minute, 'and have you got anything to do with this?'

He motioned back to the waterlogged ground which, although it didn't look like a lake anymore, was making the men's wellies sink quite deeply into the watery mud. Max gulped but held his head up high to answer him.

'Don't be stupid,' sneered Max 'do you think I did a rain dance and ordered a storm specially to flood it out?' Joe cringed and put his hood up hoping it would hide him in case the man made a lunge for him. Some of the other men were laughing at what Max had said which only annoyed the man more.

'Stupid? Stupid am I?' he advanced on Max who backed up against the nearest tree. 'We'll see who's stupid now shall we? I'm telling you to stay away from here cos this is private property. Belongs to Cheetingham's see'

He pointed with one finger to the 'C' logo on his safety hat which he replaced self-importantly on to his head. Max saw red.

'This place belongs to us, the people of Buckton-and no-one will stop me coming here!'

The next thing he knew was rough hands against his throat and his head was banged so hard against the tree behind him that he couldn't think straight for a moment. He could feel the man's fat fingers closing around his neck and his eyes tried hard to focus on the others. Cait had started screaming and trying to pull the man off and Joe was standing with his hands over his eyes as if it would make it all go away.

Suddenly there was a whooshing noise and an arrow embedded itself into the tree about a foot above Max's head but which knocked the man's helmet askew. Max could feel Cait's arms dragging him away and he collapsed in a heap on the mud. Out of still-unfocused eyes he watched the brutish thug of a workman gingerly checking the arrow. The man turned towards the puzzled faces looking at him.

'It's a trick, that's all' he shouted 'More stupid kids.'

With that there was a low thud and Max saw the man stagger backwards as another arrow grazed past his ear and split the first arrow in two lengthways. The man's eyes met Max's and he started shaking with anger. He took a step in the children's direction while Cait tried to shield Joe and the still dazed Max as best she could.

Twa-a-ang!

Another arrow whizzed through the air, knocking the hard hat completely off the bully and pinning it to the tree through the middle of the 'C' logo. Everything was deathly quiet and then, just as though a spell had been broken, the workmen ran in all directions, trying to get as far away from this devil bowman as they could. The old stories of spirits in the wood must be true!

The children looked in the direction the arrows had come from as they knew it must have been Robin who had loosed them. There was no sign of him. Max pulled himself up and they ran down with difficulty over the boggy ground, over to the bank of trees which bordered Gisburn's field. Nothing! More disappointed than they were prepared to admit, they made their way out of the wood and back along the path towards their farmhouse, Max still rubbing his neck. Joe shouted 'Look!' and they swung round in the direction he was pointing. Robin stood at the very edge of the wood watching them silently. Slowly he lifted his bow above his head in a salute and before they could wave back, he disappeared back into the wood.

'He worries me' said Cait as they walked back home, 'Sometimes he acts like a mischievous child and other times he seems very lost. Lonely even.'

'Whatever he is, he's here to help us so if he wants to be on his own occasionally, it's up to him.' said Max seriously. Cait nodded wisely, casting a concerned glance towards her big brother who now seemed to have recovered.

'The dam had gone' piped up Joe and they both looked at him.

'They must know that someone has sabotaged it,' said Max, 'that's why they have people up here now trying to cut the trees down even before the planning has been granted. They don't want any more delays like that. Although I think Robin has scared the living daylights out of them for now. I don't know how long it will keep them away though.'

Cait looked furtively at Max. She had been really scared that the man was going to hurt him even more back there. She was beginning to think they had taken more on than they could manage.

'Are you okay?' she ventured.

'Me? Of course I am.' He laughed sounding much braver than he actually felt.

*

Meanwhile at Cheetingham Manor, Albert Gisburn was shouting furiously into the phone.

'How long then? The end of the week? What? All right. Now look here, we are going to start cutting those trees down then, whether the ground is ready or not. There is no need for anyone to know as it is my land and the council have just about given their permission. The paper they are waiting for regarding the common land won't be found, it has *never* been found, so we will have no problems. We need to work fast though because as soon as the townspeople get to know, they will start their delaying tactics again. What? Never mind the solicitors and Archmount, I pay them well to keep their noses out and make things easy for me. Spirits? What on earth are you talking about man?! There are no woodland spirits – you were shot at by some idiot in league with those dratted kids. Just Get On With It!' he screamed down the phone, turning purple with rage.

The truth was, if the people found any other way to delay the building, then there was a possibility that he wouldn't have his club after all. If they were confronted with a wood that was almost devoid of trees, there was nothing they could do about it. Of course, they didn't know that there would be no jobs for local people. The leisure

85

club which he had plans for would have professional people working there up from London. It would be a place where he could conduct his very dodgy business deals in peace. It would be an exclusive club with membership only which meant that none of the townspeople would be accepted there, even if they wanted to – which he doubted.

Albert Gisburn smiled, a grin spreading across his fat face as he thought how gullible these stupid people of Buckton were. How he could make them do whatever he wanted because they were too weak. No, his plan was fool- proof, nothing could stop him now.

He reached forward and happily poured himself a measure of his favourite whisky and with his glass to his lips; he turned to look out of the window. What on earth were *they*?! Those things in the field in front of his house? He nearly choked as he swallowed the whisky and the glass flew out of his hands, crashing onto the oak floor. He crept towards the window unable to take it all in. Just shadows, like the one he had seen in the wood. Insubstantial, like negatives from old photos that had appeared in front of him but they were all shapes and sizes. As he peered tentatively he saw an extremely large shadow next to a small one, a slim one next to a fat one echoing his own figure. They were all facing Cheetingham Manor in a shimmering line. The thought entered his head that these shadows were the spirits of the wood his men had been so scared of – and they were all coming for him!

He turned and ran with a high-pitched shriek out of the office door and into the hallway where he bumped into his butler Charters.

'Stop them Charters – stop them! They're coming for me, don't let them get me! Get rid of them!'

Charter's gaze followed his master's disappearing bulk up the stairs until he heard the slamming of his bedroom door and the key being turned in the lock. His puzzled face now began to display curiosity and he gently pushed open the door of the office and looked around.

Nothing. Nothing here at all. He looked out of the window just in case but there was nothing there either. What was Master Albert going on about? Not for the first time, Charters worried that his master was away with the fairies.

CHAPTER 10

It was just striking 10.30 from the clock on top of the church tower as Max, Cait and Joe walked up the path to the thick oak doors of the church. The church itself was on the edge of the town, midway between Cheetingham Manor and the Cooper's farm. It was hidden from the town by a wooded copse which surrounded it. It was said that the copse had once been part of Robbers' Wood, the edge of which could be seen further up the hill, until that part of the wood had been cut down for timber long ago.

The door creaked open as Max put his shoulder to it. They walked towards Rev Rowley who stood smiling at them near the altar.

'Now, what's all this about' beamed the reverend 'How do you think I can help you?'

'We think you can help us to stop the Gisburn's club being built. We don't know how exactly – not yet...' Cait began to feel unsure of herself.

'Goodness me!' replied Rowley 'How on earth do you think I can do that? Not that I wouldn't love to help but I can't see how?' He smiled resignedly at them. There was a short, awkward pause then Joe broke the silence.

'You've *got* to help us, Robin Hood said you would!'

His brother and sister turned horrified eyes on him and Max threw him a warning glance.

'R-Robin...?' faltered Rev Rowley and again there was an awkward silence. Just then a voice came from behind them.

'You're not going to disappoint the children are you Rowley?'

The children turned round expectantly but instead of Robin; they saw Gisburn's solicitor, Scatlock who had been at the meeting. Max turned away from him in disgust as the man walked up to them.

'Well, if I can help, I'm sure…' Rowley broke off, 'Forgive me, this is William Scatlock. He came to ask for some advice. Do you think we can help them William?'

'I think' began Scatlock slowly and Max noticed the infuriating smile starting to spread across his face 'that at this moment, stopping the building works would be like shovelling snow in a blizzard – impossible!'

Max turned on him, his dislike of the man making him bold.

'You would say that wouldn't you? I bet you're pleased it's happening aren't you? You will get a load of money from Gisburn to make sure he can get rid of Robbers' Wood – *Our* wood'

Scatlock's eyebrows shot up in surprise.

'Well actually…'

'Well actually…' another voice echoed from the doorway as Robin stood there silhouetted against the daylight behind him.

'Actually, you'll find that's wrong. In fact if I'm any judge, you'll find it is the complete opposite of what he thinks.' Robin's long strides soon brought him up to where the others were standing 'Isn't that right Will?'

The others looked at him in amazement, including Rev Rowley whose mouth had fallen open.

'Will, you look so much like your Scatlock ancestors – and you've still got the family habit of wearing scarlet clothes eh, you popinjay?'

Scatlock at first looked shocked, then thoughtful, then very, very happy.

'Robin Hood? You don't know how much I treasure this moment. Ever since hearing my father's and grandfather's stories. They were passed down through the family for generations. We were told you helped an ancestor of ours – is that true? I knew it wasn't just a story, I knew it was the truth as neither my father nor his father was given to exaggeration and hadn't the imagination to make it up. There was no reason for them to tell me unless they thought I ought to know for the future. I've never stopped believing I would meet you one day - when the town was in trouble again. The people of Buckton have always believed in the legend – and in you.'

The two stepped forward and clasped hands as the children's' mouths fell open as far as the reverend's.

'I suppose' said Robin looking down at them 'that I owe you an explanation – and Roly Poly here.'

'How did you know that was my nickname?' said a surprised Rev Rowley while Joe stifled a giggle.

'I didn't. It was a guess but I would say that the major clue is the size of your stomach, wouldn't you?

Max held his breath at Robin's rudeness until after a few seconds he realised that the wheezing noise coming from Rowley was him laughing like a sort of deflating balloon. This set them all off laughing until Robin motioned for them all to sit down. It was time for business.

'Perhaps, as a man of the church, you can explain to these youngsters the truth of the matter' said Robin as they sat on the hard wooden pews.

'I would my dear boy but I really have no idea what is going on here.'

Robin looked across at three very expectant faces and one flustered one.

'Right, perhaps I had better explain now briefly. I met Will's ancestor when he asked for help, as he said. Originally though I knew another of Will's ancestors, also called Will, so many years ago, you wouldn't believe'

'The eldest son has always been called Will, throughout the generations.' Will said proudly. Robin smiled.

'And how many generations? Twenty or more? Your direct ancestor was a good friend and an invaluable member of my band. We used to call him Scarlet because of his habit of wearing clothes of the brightest red hue.'

Will looked down at his waistcoat and laughed.

'Will Scarlet!' whispered Max so quietly that only Cait could hear. He felt ashamed at hating this man but then he thought about the deeds and about Will's actions on behalf of Gisburn.

'Why is he on Gisburn's side then?' he blurted out.

'I think I can explain that' said Rev Rowley. 'I happen to know that Will is very much opposed to this development. He used to play in those woods when he was a child too, just like you. Yet when Gisburn came up with those deeds which had apparently been passed down from Gisburn's ancestors - some of who were Sheriffs of this county - Will saw that being in with Gisburn meant he could keep an eye on him. If there was anything illegal, he would be able to stop the planning.'

'The wicked sheriff who tried to kill Robin Hood!' breathed Joe who was listening in a sort of trance. Max and Cait wanted to laugh at him but felt, uncomfortably, that he was right.

'Absolutely.' agreed Robin, confirming their suspicions.

'But what about Rev Rowley?' ventured Max 'What has he got to do with it?'

'I think I can answer that as things are becoming much clearer now, correct me if I'm wrong' Rowley replied, looking across at Robin. 'The keepers of this church throughout its existence, each undertook a sacred vow that they would protect the town and the people of Buckton and the woods and land that surround it against any threat. It is a secret vow, belonging to this church only and which I had to swear to in God's name. If we are to believe the very strange things you have just told us – and I suppose I will have to - I believe your Friar Tuck could have been the first incumbent of the church?'

'Perhaps.' smiled Robin enigmatically.

'When we are sworn in to St. Stephen's, we are told the secret of our pledge and also, more importantly, the secret of the awakening of a mysterious figure who helps us whenever we are in desperate need. Forgive me,' he said, looking downcast 'but I thought it was a myth and until now, as did many of the other churchmen. I didn't believe it.'

'Understandable' grinned Robin stretching his long legs out in front of him 'but now I must tell you why we are all gathered here and why it is important that my orders are carried out. You, my friends, will have to be my modern-day Merry Men! Apologies my dear but I suppose you can be a Merry Maid instead!'

He was laughing at Cait's affronted expression and then at the gratified smile she gave him, before he went on.

'I have to ask difficult but not impossible things of you all. As I have told Max, Cait and Joe, you will all have to help yourselves too. You,' he said pointing at Rev Rowley 'must do whatever it takes to go as far back as you can in the church records. There is something in the back of my mind about these woods and I would like you to try and confirm it. Anything about charters to the town of Buckton, deeds concerning the woods or just records from the church itself.'

'I most certainly will, although I think all church records are kept at the city of York now. Can I ask what I am looking for specifically?'

Robin frowned and said,

'I'm not sure myself yet but all I can say is that you will know when you see it. It should mention the woods – I don't want to get your hopes up then let you down.' he finished, leaving Rowley more puzzled than ever. Nevertheless, he stood up and faced Robin.

'I promise you I will do all in my power to find this document you talk of, if it still exists.' said Rowley in a very un-Rowley voice. The children had never seen him so serious.

'You, Will' Robin looked at Will who stood up and bowed low with a flourish, indicating that Robin's word was his command. Robin grinned.

'I want you to delay the destruction of these woods, in any way and by any means, legal or illegal. If you can disprove Gisburn's claim to own the woods then so much the better.'

'I have grave doubts about those deeds.' replied Will. 'I have been in contact with a man who may be able to tell if it is a forgery and am leaving to see him tomorrow, taking the deeds with me. Gisburn thinks I have them for safe-keeping. It will also give me the greatest personal pleasure to stop Gisburn. We have more than one score to settle.'

Robin asked what he had done, as he himself had a similar score to settle.

'My father' replied Will, 'died when I was sixteen. Walter Gisburn, Albert's father, made his life a misery after my father won the battle over the destruction of the Wolfshead Tree.'

'*Our* Tree?' said Max, surprised.

'Yes' replied Will 'My father was the solicitor hired to stop Walter Gisburn cutting the tree down as he said it was dangerous and decayed – which it wasn't. There was a story going round at the time that Walter was superstitious about the tree and believed it had always brought bad luck to the Gisburns but of course, he wouldn't admit to that weakness, so he pretended he was doing it for the safety of the townspeople. My father got experts to prove that the tree was perfectly safe and also that Gisburn had tried to bribe them to say it wasn't safe. After Walter Gisburn lost the case, he never left my father alone. Somehow he persuaded my father's big clients to desert him one by one so that in the end he had no money to provide for his family, no business and no hope. I believe he died of a broken heart.'

Will looked so miserable now that Max felt doubly bad for thinking that he was the enemy. He watched as Robin sprung up and put a hand on Will's shoulder.

'I wish he had asked for help, perhaps I could have…anyway, better not to dwell on that. We'll beat Gisburn.' he said, his voice echoing round the cold grey stone of the church, 'Robbers' Wood will be safe once more and we will have our revenge on Gisburn and the whole of his rotten ancestors.'

Silence fell on the little company gathered there but a grim determination was written on each of their faces. Gisburn must not win!

CHAPTER 11

The youngest members of the Cooper family were all sitting on the big rag-rug on the kitchen floor in front of a log fire. It was a foggy day outside which made them feel cold. Instead of playing outside they had asked if Ethan and Jake could come to tea and now they all felt the warm glow of the fire on their upturned faces as they listened to Mr. Cooper.

'This farm has been in our family as far back as I can remember. The name Cooper and the name Scatlock are ancient names in this district, going way back. The first Scatlock son to be born was always called William.'

'What about *my* grandfather?' asked Ethan.

'And mine' asked Jake.

Mr. Cooper sighed.

'I really think you should be asking your own families about this but…yes, I do believe they are all originally from this town. It's a small town; everyone tends to know everyone else. That's how your fathers and I knew each other in the first place.

Unfortunately the Gisburns have always lived around here too – and have always been the same money-grabbing, nasty and downright stupid people for all that time too. As you can tell by the latest Gisburn, Albert.

Cheetingham Manor was called Buckton Hall originally but was changed to Cheetingham Manor on the orders of Connie, Albert's grandmother, the rather bossy heiress his grandfather had married for her money. She poured lots of her own money into the place and wanted it named after her in repayment.

'Walter, Albert's father, had for some reason, taken against the Wolfshead Tree. Rumour was that he had found some old papers and because of what was in these, thought that this particular tree brought bad luck to the Gisburn family. Silly superstition but there's no other reason for him suddenly wanting the tree declared unsafe and scheduling it to be felled as soon as possible.'

Max silently wondered if it was anything to do with the legend of Robin, who had been a thorn in the Gisburns' side many years ago. He also thought his father was looking decidedly shifty, not a look you would normally associate with him so he took the plunge and asked –

'Why do *you* think he wanted the Wolfshead Tree felled?'

Mr. Cooper looked uncomfortable but being an honest man said,

'These rumours surrounding the tree and his family were definitely uppermost in his mind along with the legends attached to it which we had all heard.'

Everyone on the rug glanced at each other out of the corners of their eyes.

'But the story we were all told and which had been passed down by an old woman whose family had always lived in Buckton, was that one of the Gisburn children had gone missing. I'm talking over a hundred years ago now. There was a big search organised among the workers of the

102

Buckton Hall Estate. Eventually, as night started to fall they found him.' Mr. Cooper paused and looked down. 'Tied to the Wolfshead Tree and bawling his eyes out. It seems that Walter had heard this story about his grandfather too and now was intent on destroying the tree'

This information didn't have the effect he thought it would and it was all he could do to stop everyone laughing and speak again.

'Now come on' he pleaded 'It can't have been a very pleasant experience for a young boy.'

'Yes but he must have done something bad, Mr. Cooper, for someone to have tied him up in the first place?' ventured Jake.

'You really should be asking your own fathers…'

'Dad!!' came Cait's authoritative voice.

'All right, all right. Remember this is an old story, passed down through families – and might not be the whole truth. It could just be one of those mythical stories I include in my books.

The story was that the lad in question had been bullying the other lads in the town. Anyway, he apparently   delighted in torturing them both physically and mentally. He was the school bully and was really disliked.'

'Then I don't blame them for tying him up in the least!' Max snarled 'He only got what was coming to him and he's going to get it again!'

They all cheered at this but then Jake spoke again. 'Who tied him up?'

They tried not to look at each other. Over a hundred years ago? That would be around the time Robin last appeared.

Mr. Cooper smiled.

'Young Gisburn had come across a boy walking in the wood. He had bullied this boy for years and the poor lad was terrified of him. He was carrying a trumpet of some sort that he'd just found; I believe. As Gisburn came towards him to take it, the young lad blew the thing right in his face, nearly deafening him with it, which made him doubly annoyed.

This Gisburn was delighted to find a coil of rope which had miraculously appeared in front of a tree – and decided there and then to tie the lad to it and leave him there. Suddenly, out of the corner of his eye, he saw someone step from behind the tree.

Before he could do anything, the rope was grabbed from his hand and the   stranger held Gisburn against the tree. Then he handed the rope over to the other boy so that he could have the pleasure of making this bully as scared as he himself had been.

The stranger them made sure the rope was secure and hurried the other lad off home with strict instructions not to say anything – and a threat to Gisburn that if he revealed anything, he and his men would come and get him in the middle of the night. Obviously it worked as Gisburn was too scared to reveal who it was.'

Everyone had huge grins on their faces and Joe was cheering loudly. They each, without saying anything, thought this young lad who was being bullied, must have been the ancestor of Will Scatlock's that Robin had helped. Then Max narrowed his eyes.

'Who was this stranger, the one who tied Gisburn up?'

'I really don't know. He was never found even though the lad's father really wanted to find him and thank him. He said later that he had found him but didn't tell anyone who it was so no-one knew his name.'

'Come on Dad, you know more than you're letting on.'

Mr. Cooper looked sharply at his son and realised now how much he had grown up.

'The rumour was that he might have been called Robin somebody.' he said matter-of-factly.

They all looked at each other knowingly. 'But don't go getting any ideas of these old legends of Robin Hood helping the town when it's in peril. Remember, I know my folk tales and that's all it is. We all know it's just a legend don't we?'

Mr. Cooper didn't look as though he believed his own words.

'No' said Max, looking his father straight in the eye, 'No – we don't.'

*

Reverend Rowley was up to his ears in musty old documents. He had made excuses to the Dean of York Minster and was now in a dark and dingy room just off the crypts below the Minster. He put aside the document he had been looking at and pulled out another. A cloud of dust escaped and he coughed and spluttered before perching his glasses on the end of his nose again. Nothing about Buckton or the Wood there either.

Suddenly a small box fell off a shelf in the very corner of the tiny room. He wondered how on earth he could have dislodged it from its place but as he put it back, it caught his eye. It was rusty and battered but he could make out a large brass 'B' on the top. It could have stood for anything but somehow it drew Rowley's attention to it. He walked over to the meagre light hanging from the ceiling which hardly lit up the room at all. There was only one document inside, tied with faded ribbon which had seen better days. Trembling, he pulled it out and started to read. After a few minutes where he frowned and shook his head, he put the document in the small briefcase he had brought with him. It was very puzzling but he had a strong feeling it could help. He fervently hoped so as nothing else he had found was of any use and he offered up a prayer of thanks for the divine intervention.

*

Back at the offices of Scatlock, Bashall and Print, Will Scatlock smiled to himself. He had delayed his trip to London to verify the deeds as the colleague had been ill but who was now ready and waiting for Will to provide the documentary evidence to test for forgery. He walked over to the filing cabinet and looked under the 'G', picking out the document which Gisburn had smugly handed over to him containing the deeds which proved his ownership of Robbers' Wood. He calmly put it in a large envelope and sealed it.

Poking his nose round the main office door he saw the eager face of Elias Print, the most junior partner of the practice.

'Please can you book me into a hotel near Leadenhall Street in London for two nights Elias? I may be longer if I can't find out what I need to but I will make further arrangements then. Can I also put my trust in you and ask that if Albert Gisburn asks where his deeds are, tell him you are not sure and he will have to wait till I get back as I have taken the keys to my filing cabinets?'

Elias smiled. He knew something was going on but it didn't matter, he trusted Mr. Scatlock. That Gisburn man was so uncouth, it wouldn't hurt him to wait a while and not get his own way.

'You can rely on me' he said as Will nodded and dashed out of the door.

CHAPTER 12

In the enormous kitchen at Max's farmhouse, the chairs at the long table were filled with his father's friends. Extra chairs had been found from around the house to fit them all in. Mr. Cooper's voice cut through the hubbub.

'Does it take a child – my own son – to tell us what is right? I am proud of my lad, of course but what happened to our spirit? What happened to our sense of duty?' He leaned forward conspiratorially towards the men, 'What happened to doing right by Buckton, a town where we all grew up. I remember most of you here from school and this old town hasn't treated us too badly has it?' There were murmurs of agreement. 'We *must* fight Gisburn on this matter. Not just for our children but for their children and their children's children too. This is

109

our town, our wood we are talking about. The Gisburns have been mistrusted here for as long as any of us can remember and with good reason. I'm asking you now; can I count on you all?'

A great shout went up from the men at the table as one by one they stood up and vowed they would help.

*

Five children sat listlessly around the Wolfshead Tree. Having tried and failed to find Robin they now sat discussing what they could do next.

'Don't you think it's all in the hands of the grown-ups now Max? There's nothing we can do. You heard Robin.' Ethan looked down at the ground as he spoke, feeling as disappointed as the others looked.

For a few moments they sat there in silence despondently. Eventually Joe piped up,

'So we *are* giving up then?'

'What do you mean?' asked Max defensively.

'Well, you said in the church hall that we shouldn't give up, didn't you?' There was a pause, 'So…are we?' Joe asked with a frown.

Max clenched and unclenched his fists for a moment or two then sprang up.

'Of course we're not! You want to help? Well I've thought of something that may put Gisburn off for a while.'

He started telling them his plans in a low voice in case they were overheard by Cheetingham spies in the woods but his whispered words went much further than that.

*

A dark-haired, cornflower-blue eyed figure stood against the lilac tree outside Gisburn's window. His slim figure rested indolently against the tree but as he was watching the scene through the window, his face showed steely determination. Gisburn was on the phone yet again, his tubby figure pacing up and down his office.

'I said **NOW!**' he shouted 'First thing in the morning those trees must be cut down. I can't afford to wait any longer. DO YOU HEAR ME?'

He then appeared to be listening intently to the person on the other end of the phone, a miracle in itself. Then his face went red, then puce, and then blotchy with white mixed in.

'WHAT? Robin Hood?! Are you completely mad? There.is.no.such.thing!' he spelt out to the caller. After a short pause he screamed,

'If you can't do it, I'll find someone who can!' and slammed the phone down. This would delay things while he found other workmen and he could really, really do without this. He had tried to get the deeds back earlier so he could keep them safe and away from prying eyes but that wretched Scatlock had gone away for a couple of days and the idiot partner Print didn't know where the keys were. Things seemed to be slipping out of his grasp and it was due to this superstitious nonsense. Robin Hood indeed!

Supernatural ghosts? Legends of the wood come alive? What a load of old codswallop!

Suddenly, he stopped in his tracks and thought of those shadows he had seen, both in the wood and even here in his grounds. He tried not to think about the arrow in his hallway and the missing horn too as he looked warily around him. He held his head as high as his fat little neck would let him then walked slowly out of his office, nervously darting his eyes around the room. He could feel something in there even though he couldn't see anything and he gave a shudder before shutting the door tightly and going in to his sitting room.

Robin leant back against the lilac tree with a satisfied smile. It was happening. The tide was turning and things looked like they were going against Gisburn. A mischievous look passed over his face and he reached for something that was hanging around his neck. Moving soundlessly, as silent as a ghost, he was soon crouching under the windowsill of Gisburn's sitting room. Robin peered inside and nearly gave himself away by laughing at the sight in front of him. Gisburn was grooming his moustache in the over mantel mirror, preening, smiling and generally admiring himself. Robin put his hand tightly over his mouth to stop himself from laughing. When he dare look in the room again Gisburn was pouring a whisky from the decanter on the table and Robin watched as he settled himself down on the large leather settee. He reached for the remote control to switch the TV on and lifted the glass towards his lips.

Suddenly, there was a huge blast from Robin's hunting horn, echoing around the grounds but most especially inside Cheetingham Manor. Gisburn's eyes opened wide as he heard the dreaded noise, his glass flew up into the air and the whisky landed on his bald head, running down into his startled eyes.

Outside the window Robin was doubled up, his shoulders shaking with laughter. Of course, beating Gisburn was a serious matter but there was no reason why he shouldn't have a little fun along the way. With a spring in his step he made his way towards the woods, doing a little victory dance on the way.

*

Two days later, Gisburn was still in negotiation with the new workmen who would construct his leisure club. Things were going too slowly for his liking and he needed to get going before anyone could stop him. Not that they could of course but he wanted to make sure. He decided to take a walk up to the site before it got dark to make sure it was drying out properly. There had been no rain to speak of since that night where the torrential rain had turned the site into a quagmire. That – and the intervention of some of the townspeople of course. That dam was man-made and because of that and the rain, his land had been flooded. They wouldn't win though. It was in this determined or rather, stroppy mood, that he stomped off towards the wood to inspect his building site.

He reached the place which until a few days ago had still been muddy but it was drying out nicely now. He started prodding at the ground with one of the stakes which had been measuring out the area. Hmm, he thought, reassuringly dry and just ready to fell the trees and start digging. Enchanted woods? Ha!

As soon as the words finished forming in his mind, another wooden stake was slid quietly over his left shoulder from behind. He froze.

'Wh-who is it?' he squeaked.

'Never mind that' came an attempt at a deep voice, 'just keep walking.'

With the stake resting on his shoulder, Gisburn walked up to where the person behind him guided him. As he stumbled along, he thought that it couldn't be the townspeople as they wouldn't have the guts. He shivered slightly as the thought of those shadows filtered into his brain. Could it be them? He allowed himself to be guided deeper into the wood the stake digging uncomfortably in his back. He was a coward at heart and knew his limitations. There was no way he could try to tackle one of the townspeople and come off best. At last, they came within sight of the Wolfshead Tree.

'No!' said Gisburn. He thought of his family's own history and knew what was going to happen. He couldn't stay tied to the tree in this wood overnight. He spun round, knocking the stake to the ground at the same time. He came face to face with the terrified faces of five children. A wicked smile spread across his face.

'Kids!' he laughed 'What did you think you were going to do, torture me till I said I wouldn't cut the trees down? I don't *think* so.' and he laughed loudly, his little piggy eyes creased up with hatred.

Max saw red. He hated this man with a vengeance. All his strength and determination went into grabbing Gisburn's arms and holding them round his back. Gisburn still laughed.

'What now?' he said and broke away from Max so that he could walk away. Instead, he realised that he had absolute power over these children and he might as well make the most of it. So he stood there, laughing cruelly as they repeatedly tried and failed to keep hold of him to move him towards the tree.

'Do you really think you can destroy my plans? A few little kids?'

He leant down towards Max as he and Ethan tried to grab his arms again.

'Not even your gutless fathers can do it' he whispered.

Jake suddenly came alive.

'My father is *not* gutless' he shouted, 'he's braver than you and the rest of your stupid family!' and his small frame suddenly found great strength. Jake charged at Gisburn, his head down and his arms outstretched. Gisburn's own arms shot out and caught Jake, throwing him onto the ground. Stunned, he lay there for a few seconds as the others gathered round. Eventually, he lifted himself on one elbow and gave them a wry grin to show he was alright. Max and the rest turned towards Gisburn who was smirking as he started to walk away. Before they had the chance to do anything, there was a rustle of leaves and everything went deathly quiet. Gisburn looked nervously around him. As the rest of them watched, they saw Gisburn's eyes open wide and he threw his arm in front of him and then put his own arm up his back. The children watched in amazement as he spun round jerkily and headed back towards the tree. Gradually they saw an outline form behind Gisburn, almost like a shadow and not just one. More were appearing all the time. He heard Cait and Joe scream and he stepped over warily to where they stood and put his arms around their shoulders.

'It's okay, I know it is.' he said with conviction.

As he spoke, the shadowy creatures passed beside them and over to where Gisburn stood, terrified and shaking, against the Wolfshead Tree. One of the shadows, a very large one which towered over the others, seemed to salute Max who, to his own surprise, saluted back. The large shadow then grabbed hold of Gisburn, pulling him back against the tree. Gisburn screamed. A girly scream thought Cait, and the other shadows held him there. After a minute or two, when nothing else happened, Gisburn assumed his favourite smarmy expression and thrusting his arms out, stepped away from the tree. It was so easy. The shadow people seemed to look at each other in confusion and Gisburn laughed nervously.

'I'm going home' he declared with a tremor in his voice which made him sound squeaky. He shuffled forward a couple of steps before Max threw himself on top of him.

'Oomph!' gasped Gisburn as he and Max landed in a heap. 'That will cost you dear.'

He managed after a struggle to throw Max off and got himself into an upright position. Gisburn turned round and laughed.

'So long children and…things' he glanced briefly at the shadows and headed away from the tree towards his home.

Suddenly, there was a rush of air and a change in the atmosphere. What appeared to be a shimmering presence through the leaves turned slowly into Robin as the figure approached them.

'I'm terribly sorry' he said lightly, 'I forgot you needed this.' And he held out a coil of stout rope towards the largest of the shadows who grabbed it urgently.

'Well, come on kids' urged Robin, smiling at their incredulous faces, 'I think they may need some help.'

With that, Max, Ethan and Jake grabbed hold of the astonished Gisburn and pulled him back to the tree, aided by the shadows and Cait and Joe cheering them on. With a thud, Gisburn found himself with his back against the tree, looking up through the leaves which the wind seemed to be rustling more loudly than ever, hurting his ears.

'Let me go!' he screeched as the large shadow tied the rope round and round the portly figure. It handed over the end of the rope to Jake who, with a flourish, tied the rope so tightly that Gisburn would never get loose.

'Now' said Robin, 'perhaps we will leave him till he has learned his lesson. We'll check on him in the morning shall we?' and he stood back, watching through the trees at the darkening skies. Just before the children turned to go home, Robin bent down to whisper something in Max's ear.

CHAPTER 13

Very early next morning, the children made their way, as instructed by Robin the night before, to Robbers' Wood. Gisburn would have been tied up for nearly ten hours by now. Dawn was just breaking and they had all sneaked out of the house quietly, leaving a note saying they were having breakfast in the woods which was true in a way, although they would probably be back before they were missed.

As they neared the Wolfshead Tree the first thing they saw was smoke rising and mixing with the early morning mist. Then they could smell the tantalising aroma of bacon.

'Mmm' said Joe, his nose in the air following the smell.

Robin was there, leaning against the tree again but on the opposite side from Gisburn, who was incandescent with rage and shouting words that Cait thought Joe shouldn't hear! It was quite cool although the day was set to be warm and sunny. Max noticed the satisfied smile on Robin's face as he put his head back against the gnarled bark and listened to Gisburn's rants.

'I'll have you for this' he screamed, his fat little chins wobbling as he shook. Max couldn't tell if he was shaking with the cold or with rage.

'I'll have you all up in court and put in prison. I'll have you HANGED' he shouted at the top of his voice. He had obviously been like this all night. He turned towards the children who had just reached the tree.

'You too!' he screamed 'and your parents.'

Cait looked worried and Robin went towards her.

'Don't worry' he said gently putting his hand on Cait's shoulder 'he can't touch your parents and no-one would believe him anyway. You assisted a lot of shadows? You helped Robin Hood tie him to a tree? They'll think he's mad.'

He turned towards Gisburn who was spitting with anger and whose face looked like it would explode.

'Actually, I think they'd be right.' He laughed at Cait, who noticed that his light blue eyes crinkled up attractively under his long dark lashes and dark brows. She hadn't noticed how good-looking he was before. She blushed and mumbled her thanks before hiding behind Max.

Max was staring in wonderment at Robin's band of men. Whereas before, they had been insubstantial shadows, they now appeared more solid. Their features were more pronounced and the tall one, who he gathered was Little John from the others shouting to him, threw back his head and gave a big, booming laugh at Gisburn's plight. They almost seemed real now, Max thought. Almost but not quite. They had shimmery outlines like Robin had last night when he first appeared - and Max, for the first time, thought *Woodland Spirits*! The legends of the wood, were they true? Was this what they were?

One of the men who had been standing over the campfire turning bacon and frying eggs on a large metal grill pan, gave a nod to Robin who strode towards Gisburn.

'Now little man' he addressed the purple ball of rage in front of him, 'I'm going to be very kind and release you because we're just about to break our fast and we'd like you to join us.'

Some of the men undid the ropes with difficulty as Gisburn had struggled so hard he had actually pulled the ropes tighter against the tree. As soon as he was released and found his balance, he tried to break away in the direction of Cheetingham Manor. He suddenly found a sword pointed at his neck as Robin, as quick as lightning, jumped in front of him.

'Oh I don't think so.' Robin smiled calmly 'I'm sure you'll need a good breakfast in you after a night tied to the tree. Aren't you hungry?

Gisburn tried to say no but because of the sword tip against his neck he could only manage to squeak 'mmff'

Robin led him back slowly to where the outlaws sat in a circle, their features much plainer now than last night, and motioned for him to sit down, which he grudgingly did.

'And I think it would be incredibly bad-mannered of you to run away after we've prepared this breakfast feast to cheer you up. Don't you?' he said looking across at the children standing open-mouthed near him.

'Yes I do!' Joe managed to shout when he'd recovered his voice.

'There you are then' laughed Robin, 'Bacon, eggs, bread, a basket of fresh rosy apples too and ale to drink. It may not be your average breakfast but I guarantee it will be delicious.'

Gisburn stared resolutely ahead of him and refused the plate they waved in front of his face. Max and the boys joined the outlaws and tucked in to the feast. The bacon tasted wonderful, cooked as they had been in the open air. The eggs and the warm crusty bread disappeared as soon as they were set down on the plates. Cait, who had been thinking about going vegetarian, decided that it could wait a few days and grabbed a piece of bacon.

Gisburn's resolve wavered too as, one by one, the men waved food in front of him. Robin put some bacon between two slices of bread and handed it to him. There was a slight hesitation but then Gisburn realised that he hadn't had anything to eat since lunchtime yesterday and his stomach gave a huge gurgle. Joe laughed and then Gisburn grabbed the sandwich and wolfed it down as fast as he could, grease running down his chins as he did so. A great belch emerged from him but still he kept on eating. Robin glanced at Max and laughed silently.

When everyone had eaten their fill, they fell silent. Gisburn looked out of the corner of his eyes, one way then the other, wondering what was going to happen next. The sword was at Robin's side but even if he managed to avoid that in a dash for freedom, all the other men – they couldn't quite be called shadows now – had swords or bows laid on the ground next to them. He wouldn't get far. Robin turned towards him, shook his head and then pulled him up.

'Well, I suppose I'll have to let you go back home. First though, you have to make a promise that you will leave Robbers' Wood and the Wolfshead Tree alone and that you will never fell any trees or build anything on this land. Do you promise?'

The sword was at his throat again and Gisburn could feel the point nick his skin, causing a trickle of blood to run down his neck onto his collar. With a flash of understanding, he realised who he was actually dealing with. All the stories had been passed down through his family about this man and he had chosen not to believe them. Thinking hurriedly, he remembered tales of a wolfs-head, an outlaw. He was not a man to be messed with, for all his befriending of children, ladies in distress and doing what was right for his fellow men. Some of the stories he had heard proved how ruthless Robin Hood could be – and he was only now really starting to believe it. This was no elaborate charade designed to frighten him, it was all true – the legend was true and he realised he had known this for days. His whole body stiffened and he gulped noisily.

'I-I-I erm, I promise' he found himself saying. Joe cheered but the others kept quiet as the men still looked angrily at Gisburn. They obviously didn't trust him and he had never given them any reason to either. Robin raised one eyebrow and his mouth was set in a determined line.

'You promise then? Of course, the promise of a Gisburn is always to be relied on' he said sarcastically. 'But I suppose that will have to do for now.' He leaned forwards with a length of rope handed to him by the outlaw known as Little John, and then he tied Gisburn's wrists tightly. Then reaching behind him on his belt, his fingers closed around a dagger. He slowly pointed it at Gisburn.

The children gasped and Cait and Joe half-closed their eyes, not entirely wanting to miss out on what was happening but feeling quite scared. Robin's eyes stared unblinking into Gisburn's which were now as big as saucers. The dagger got ever nearer and it was clear that Robin was preparing to use it. Even Max was getting worried, surely he wouldn't kill Gisburn? This wasn't what they wanted at all.

Suddenly, the dagger that was aimed at Gisburn's heart was lowered and in the blink of an eye, its sharp blade had cut off the button on his trouser waistband. Another quick movement and the dagger forced the zip down. For a few seconds there was silence and then, as if in slow motion,

Gisburn's sensible tweed trousers fell down around his ankles. A great cheer went up and everyone, including the relieved children, started laughing.

Robin got hold of Gisburn's shoulders, turned him round in the direction of Cheetingham Manor and smacked him firmly across the seat of his baggy white underpants to send him on his way home. Gisburn stumbled to the edge of the wood, his trousers still flapping round his ankles and his wrists still tied and made his way across the field to his home.

Cursing, shouting and out of breath, he reached the side entrance of his house where the triple garage and orchard were. He falteringly made his way over to where Charters the butler stood at the kitchen door, open-mouthed. As Gisburn passed the chicken coop where his prize chickens were kept. Peering in, he couldn't see any of the eggs which they supplied. Looking up he saw Charters shrug his shoulders in bewilderment. As he turned back, he noticed the apple trees in his orchard didn't have half as many apples as they had yesterday. Gisburn blinked like an owl for a few seconds then a great roar erupted from him.

'Aaaaaghhh!' he shouted at the top of his voice as he realised he had been eating his own eggs and apples. He had a flash of understanding and just knew the rest of the breakfast would been taken from his own cupboards and his fridge. 'I'll get that villain back if it's the last thing I do!'

Charters watched him screaming, half undressed, in the middle of the courtyard and pityingly shook his head at the sight in front of him although the corner of his mouth twitched suspiciously as he went to help his master.

CHAPTER 14

Max felt out of his depth. Rev Rowley had asked
him to come to the church for a meeting but it was
a school day. Max felt it was important enough to
skip school for this once but was glad he didn't
have the responsibility of his friends, brother and
sister missing it too. He wondered why it was just
he who the Reverend had asked?

As he sneaked out of his house towards the
church, he wondered what use he would be at the
meeting. He had never been much good at pushing
himself forward and had been too shy to put his
point of view across properly when asked at
school. He would be the only non-grown-up person
there, although he wasn't sure that Robin actually
qualified as an adult. What could he say that would
make any difference?

Approaching the arched, oak door of the church, he felt a sense of age and times past. This building had been here, incredibly, since Robin first existed over a thousand years ago. He felt very small against the backdrop of the mellowed stone church with its castellated tower. He pushed open the door to find there was no-one there.

'Hello' he shouted, his voice echoing around the vaulted roof to be met with silence. He stood there for a minute or two before the door behind him opened again. Will stood there grinning and for once, Max was pleased to see him.

'No-one else here yet?' he asked 'is Robin late?'

'...and here I am, right on cue' came an amused voice and Robin swung down from behind the pulpit.

'That's what I call an entrance' called Rev Rowley as he stepped through the open door behind Will.

They all sat down on the red carpet in front of the altar with the light of the stained-glass window behind it making coloured patterns on the floor. Robin leaned forward.

'We are here to see what information we have gathered and how far we have got with acting on it since we last met. I'm assuming that you Max will tell your friends and family so they know what is happening?'

Robin smiled and nodded at Max as he spoke and Max felt ridiculously proud to have been singled out to be the spokesman for the children.

'Firstly' Robin continued 'and you will not be in the least surprised - Albert Gisburn has not kept his word.'

Max scowled and the others allowed themselves a grim half smile.

'There was always the faint hope that he would see the error of his ways, especially when scared half to death and threatened but he ran true to form, going straight to Will to get things moving even faster. I'll let Will tell you all about it.'

Will put his head down for a moment and mumbled,

'I told him I would see to it straight away.'

'What?' shouted Max, jumping up 'didn't you at least try to stand up to him?

Robin motioned silently with his arm for Max to sit down and then nodded at Will to continue.

'I had to pretend to go along with it ' Will said, turning to look at Max 'because I have something else I didn't want him to find put about. I didn't want to raise his suspicions.'

'…and what didn't you want him to find out about?'

'That I have applied for an extension of planning notice on behalf of the people of Buckton. It's quite legal and will give us another few days before Gisburn manages to overrule it as no doubt he will. He has friends in high places'

Max winced as he remembered those exact words coming from Gisburn's mouth at the start of all this.

'By that time though' Will continued 'I hope his document of ownership of the woods will be back from London. I had to leave it there for tests. If, as Gisburn claims, that document is hundreds of years old then these tests will either prove or disprove it.'

'Then we have him!' smiled Robin.

'Well, technically yes but we really need to prove the common land and right of way granted to the townspeople. We need to find that charter. It should have been either with the town officials or in the church vaults. Just in case the ownership document Gisburn has given us is forged, I have a list of people who might have had the expertise to forge them for Gisburn. I am going through them and making enquiries.'

'Well done Will. Now you Roly Poly' and Robin smiled affectionately at the Reverend who grinned back.

'Well as you know, I went to York Minster where our church documents are now kept and I found a box of papers dealing with the diocese of Buckton showing all the dealings with this church and the parish of Buckton for hundreds of years. Unfortunately' he looked so downcast that Max felt sorry for him 'the only document which mentioned the woods ownership was when it still belonged to the church in 1297. We know it passed out of the church's hands after that as there are a few references to the wood being 'previously' owned by the church but nothing about who actually does own them now.'

'So we can't prove the woods are not Gisburn's then unless his document is proved false? asked Will.

'Well' said Rowley mysteriously 'there was something…'

He and Robin exchanged glances.

'I found an old box with 'B' inscribed on it. When I looked inside there was a document marked 'St Stephen's Church, Buckton'. When I opened it there were words which seem to be from an old hymn or song. I have it here.'

He reached into a bag next to him on the ground and brought out some sheets of A4 paper.

'Not the original of course, I had to leave it in York for safekeeping but I copied it out word for word and then made four copies of that – one for each of us.'

Again, as Rowley handed them out, Max swelled with pride at being included in this important meeting. When he glanced down at the sheet of paper though, he looked puzzled.

'It doesn't make any sense!'

'Makes perfect sense to me' Robin laughed 'I will read it for you.'

He read in low tones the verse that was written on the paper. It sounded like a foreign language to Max.

'It's in Old English, my English when I was born. It's a poem and I will do my best to translate it for you, as near as I can'

At this, Will took a pen out from his pocket and turned the sheet of paper over so he could write down the translation. Immediately, Rowley and Max did the same. Max gave Rowley a pen from his school pencil case. Robin, struggling a little with some of the translation, read out the verse in words they could understand.

'Where the hill meets the stream and the deer leads the herd,

Far below in the darkness where only the casks lie,

They wait next to Brimstone, Salt and Fire,

Guarded by the ancient tree's namesake,

To be delivered up by God's mercy to the holy church

Then order shall be restored to Bocheton and its people

And deeds will be shown for the right.'

There was a short pause then Max spoke up

'It doesn't even rhyme!'

'Well it did in Old English' shot back Robin, looking a trifle hurt.

They all looked at each other, frowning.

'Does anyone have any idea what any of it means?' asked Robin. 'Rowley?'

'Now it has been translated, it does seem to have something to do with Buckton and the church. Bocheton is the old name for Buckton.'

'I think' said Will 'that the verse is like a treasure trail to help us find the document. I think that if we can solve this, then we have found Buckton's Common Land law for the woods.'

Max looked excited for a second then frowned again.

'If none of us knows what it means though, how will we ever find it?'

'Here's what I want you to do' Robin said 'take these copies and the translations you have written down and see what you can find out. Rowley, look through all the church records you still have here and the library records to see if anything helps. For instance, does 'casks' mean caskets? As in coffins buried in the churchyard?

Will, look through the legal documents as far back as you can go to see if anything is mentioned about a herd of deer or Bocheton.

Max, ask your family and their friends, whose ancestors have lived around here for hundreds of years, if they recognise any of the places or things mentioned in the verse.'

Max nodded wisely, he thought his father, as a local historian, might be able to help him. He couldn't think though of the explanation of how he got the verse. He folded his paper up neatly and one by one they left the church, although Max didn't see where Robin disappeared to. He was worried that he would get found out about staying off school but nothing now seemed as important as saving Robbers' Wood. When he thought of the history of that place, of the church, the town and the families themselves who had lived there for generations, when he thought about the myths set around the woods and the magic that he now knew was in them, he was determined that an odious little man such as Gisburn should not spoil the legend that was Robbers' Wood or cut down the

139

mystical Wolfshead Tree. He suddenly stopped short, clutching the paper. Gisburn thought the Tree brought bad luck to his family and would be determined to cut it down but it was Robin's entry into this world and his exit from it. If the tree was cut down, what would happen to Robin? Without Robin, who would guard the town of Buckton and its woods?

CHAPTER 15

Albert Gisburn was annoyed. In fact, he was *very* annoyed. If truth were told he was absolutely fuming. He had been called before a meeting of the planning committee in the nearby town of Sherburn where the district council offices were. Called before them like some criminal appearing before a judge! He stopped buttoning his jacket up and chuckled to himself. Charters, who was standing behind him after handing him the jacket, nearly jumped out of his skin. It wasn't a sound he was used to hearing from his bad-tempered boss. As Gisburn turned round quickly to grab his briefcase, Charters jumped again and backed away.

'What's wrong with you man, you look like you've seen a ghost?!' Gisburn shouted then remembering, he turned slowly around to check the hallway in case there were any 'shadows' scaring the butler. Nothing.

With a 'hmmf' he wobbled out of the door as fast as his fat legs would carry him. He allowed himself a self-satisfied smile which, if Charters had seen it, would have sent him scurrying for the safety of the kitchen. No, they couldn't stop him now. Everything was arranged for next Monday because by then he would have heard news of the planning permission. He knew it would be in his favour as he had three people on the planning committee who he had 'bought' with favours or money. He had a huge team of over a hundred men armed with chainsaws and axes, all ready to chop down the trees in one fell swoop and in one full day from dawn until dusk. It had taken almost a military operation to arrange this and he was thankful he wouldn't have to do it all again. In under a week the trees would be cut down, including that cursed Wolfshead Tree, and his club would be built. He hurried to his car, prising himself in behind the steering wheel. He had hired the best legal brain and was meeting him at the planning offices. He would run rings around them!

*

Will Scatlock clutched his briefcase tightly to his chest. The proof he had been expecting had not yet arrived from London and his enquiries about forgers had not turned up anything either so there was not much he could do today and he knew it.

'Ah, Scatlock!' bellowed Gisburn, 'let's get this over with, it shouldn't take long.

Will closed his eyes and crossed his fingers behind his back. The planning committee sat on one side of a long wooden table and looked unsmilingly at Gisburn and Will as they entered the room.

'Now sir' said a gaunt-looking man, 'we are to understand that there are further objections to your leisure club and extra time has been applied so we can go through these objections again. Are you aware of this?'

'Of course I'm aware man' screamed Gisburn going red in the face, 'why else do you think I'd be wasting my time here? I'm sure we can forget about that, can't we? Scatlock phoned me about it this morning.'

The committee chairman looked quickly at Will, who looked away. Of course, he would know

143

it was Will himself who put the objection in but luckily he said nothing to Gisburn, he just sat back with a steely expression on his face.

At that point, an oily-haired man, dandruff showing on the shoulders of his black jacket, addressed Gisburn with a smile. Oh no, thought Will, he's actually bowing to him!

The man was indeed bowing and nodding to Gisburn who seemed even more annoyed than usual.

'I would just like to say' said the oily man, 'that Mr Gisburn has been a pillar of society round these parts for many years.

Gisburn visibly relaxed as he remembered that this man was hoping for the manager's job at his club. He wouldn't get it of course but he wasn't going to let him know that while he could be of some use. He attempted a smile that was more like a snarl; making Will step away from him nervously.

'Mr.Gisburn, moreover,' the oily man continued, 'is a charitable benefactor to many well-deserving places around the town. The lifeboat, children's home and old folk's home have received donations from him (fifty pence in the tin when they were collecting, thought Gisburn happily to himself) and there have been many donations to the council for trips abroad as goodwill ambassadors…' he looked along the line of councillors, most of who were looking at their feet or shuffling uncomfortably as they remembered the free holidays they had taken advantage of – Gisburn had them over a barrel.

'…and of course, with Mr.Gisburn's scheme, he would be creating jobs for many local people.'

The row of faces at the table reluctantly nodded at this. Will scowled, Gisburn had made it seem like they owed him and it may just work to his advantage. Were they all in his pay?

Gisburn was concealing a nasty grin. Local people? Did he really think he would employ the small-town, unsophisticated inhabitants of Buckton in his exclusive club? He had already found his staff in London, although he wasn't going to let them know this just now of course.

After five minutes of whispered discussion and note-passing from the committee, it was agreed that if no other objections were received, the building plans could go ahead after the objection time had lapsed.

Everyone started packing up as Gisburn looked at Will urgently. Will pretended he had no idea what he meant. Gisburn whispered very loudly in his ear making Will pull away and with a heavy heart he asked,

'Does this mean the original planning document stands with no extension because of the objection? Sunday at midnight?'

The steely-eyed man, who had first spoken and then remained silent, turned to face them.

'It will have to be extended to Monday afternoon so we can meet again to ensure all is well.'

'But, th…you can't…Monday…?' spluttered Gisburn, his eyes sticking out of his head as he stared venomously at the oily man who had helped him but he was already sneaking away towards the door.

'Mr Gisburn' said the steely-eyed man with authority so that Gisburn stopped to look at him, 'I'm sure that one day won't make any difference to your plans. I myself hoped that some document or objection would turn up to stop the building but if it hasn't then Monday afternoon at 2pm it is. That will be our final meeting. I expect you to be here.' And with that he walked stiffly out of the door.

Gisburn hissed at Will through his teeth.

'Fat lot of good you were. I don't know what I'm paying you an extortionate amount of money for. Standing there like a frightened rabbit.'

There was some reason why Gisburn was annoyed at the Monday afternoon ruling and Will wanted to find out why. If only those papers would arrive. Will thought quickly.

'It's like he said, one day won't make any difference will it? It's not as if you would start chopping trees down before the planning is granted is it?' he laughed nervously.

'Isn't it? ISN'T IT?!' shouted Gisburn leaning right up to Will's face. He suddenly seemed to come to his senses. He couldn't really trust Scatlock – he could see he took after his father – a do-gooder.

'Chop the trees down before that?' Gisburn scoffed unconvincingly, 'whatever gave you that idea?'

Will watched him waddle out of the building. He scowled, deep in thought, and then hurried off urgently in search of Robin.

CHAPTER 16

'Dad?' ventured Max, watching his father's head bent over his books at the table. His father was a local historian and it was an all-consuming hobby as well as his living. He was so engrossed he didn't hear Max until he repeated it.

'Yes?' he said, looking up quickly. It was obvious he hadn't heard him come in.

'You know a lot about the history of these parts don't you?'

'Actually' his father smiled 'I'm trying to use that knowledge to find something that might stop Gisburn at the moment. My friends and I are searching every possible book or reference for help'

'Then this might help – if you can tell me what it means? It's from an Old English poem. Don't lose it will you?' Max whispered as he handed the translation to his father.

Mr. Cooper read it through quickly and sat back.

'Well what is it? It reads like some sort of treasure hunt?' he asked, puzzled.

'I suppose it is really' answered Max and then he sighed. He might as well tell his father the truth. Well, the parts he would believe anyway.

'It's a translation of a poem that is centuries old. We, that is the Reverend Rowley and me, think that if we can work out where the poem is talking about, it may lead us to the lost deeds that will prove that the people of Buckton own the right of way through the woods.'

George Cooper looked at his son in astonishment.

'I'm surprised Reverend Rowley has taken you into his confidence. Where did you say he found this?'

'That's just a translation from the Old English; the original document is still in York Minster vaults.'

His father looked impressed.

'I think that what we may find is not just a right of way but a document to show that Robbers' Wood was given to the people of Buckton by the church and has never been owned by Gisburn. That is what I was looking for just now as these old books seem to offer up evidence of the church keeping such a document at some point. You say there was nothing else at York Minster? No more documents?'

'Just that poem in an old box'

'Let's have a look. If you're sure it's been translated from the Old English properly?' he looked enquiringly at Max 'It really needs an expert'

'We- erm- found one' said Max, suppressing a grin.

'Where the casks lie?' Mr. Cooper was scanning the paper, 'That could mean the crypts in the churchyard? Coffins were quite often called caskets. Gisburn's family crypt? It could be. Let me see, Brimstone salt and fire? That doesn't go in a crypt – although Fire and Brimstone is what some of the old priests used to preach – visions of hellfire if you didn't repent your sins and suchlike. Safe inside the Ancient Tree's namesake. The only trees in the churchyard are yews although there are a few beech trees planted on the outside of the walls. Beech? Yew?'

He looked puzzled but Max knew that he loved to get involved in a local mystery and was excited about this. He moved round so he could read the paper his father was holding.

'It looks like we have to give the document to the church? The deeds show the right of way?'

'I think perhaps it was the church that hid them in the first place, knowing the reputation of Gisburn's ancestors. Things weren't like they are now – done mostly by committees and councils, even if they were supposed to be. Unscrupulous people, like the Gisburns, were not above taking things by force and if that meant killing people along the way, then so be it. It may not just be the right of way' he continued, staring at the paper, 'it may be that is our right or that it just is…right?'

Max could see his father was immersed in the mystery and started to back towards the door. His father suddenly came round.

'Okay' he said 'Leave it with me and I'll see what I can do.'

Max shut the door quietly behind him and decided to go and find Robin to see whether he had discovered anything yet. Cait and Joe were probably still in town with his Mum so instead of going up towards the woods he decided to walk down towards the road to call for Ethan first. Unfortunately, Ethan was being dragged out by his mother to get a new pair of shoes and as Max left he could see Ethan pulling gloomy faces from the back of the car as they drove off.

From Ethan's house, it was easier to cut up by the side of Cheetingham Manor to the woods and as Max thought he had wasted enough time already, he decided to go that way. He cut through the gap in the trees and then kept to the other side of the hedge that bordered the Cheetingham estate, so he wouldn't be seen. As he passed by Cheetingham Manor, he found a small gap in the hedge and couldn't resist peeping through. He found he was above the courtyard where Albert

Gisburn kept his pigs. He thought he saw a movement in the courtyard and poked his head further through the hedge to see Gisburn overseeing the delivery of some new chickens. He directed the men to take them out of the van and deposit them in the chicken run, firmly dropping the wire lid on them so they couldn't escape. As the van drove off, Max saw Gisburn look proudly at his new acquisitions.

Suddenly, there was a furious beating of wings as a large black bird flew swiftly across to Gisburn and started flapping in front of his face. Max's eyes opened wide as he recognised Charlie Crow, Robin's occasional companion. Gisburn quickly put his stubby little arms up to shield his face and tried to run inside but the crow kept flapping directly in front of him, stopping Gisburn's escape to the safety of his house. It was hard to work out who was screeching louder, Charlie or Gisburn, as the crow blocked his every move.

Max noticed a movement to his right and as he glanced over, he noticed a figure slowly appearing from behind the pig pen wall. Robin! Max grinned and watched with added interest. He saw Robin move silently across to the chicken run where

Gisburn's new prize possessions were. Max looked to make sure Gisburn couldn't see him but realised that Charlie Crow was distracting his attention away from Robin on purpose. All Gisburn wanted to do was reach that house and had his back turned to Robin. Max watched Robin who lifted up the top-opening door in the chicken run and lifted out some eggs. The chickens, who just having got used to their new home were making a loud fuss at being so rudely disturbed. At this. Gisburn tried to turn his head but Charlie swooped on him again, making him duck his head down and throw his arms over his bald head.

Robin ran straight in Max's direction. Max had the strange feeling that he knew he was there, crouched behind the hedge. Just before he got there, he turned towards Charlie and gave him a signal, pointing towards the pig pen.

At this, Charlie started flying towards Gisburn in short bursts, making him back up towards the pig pen, although this was the exact opposite direction in which Gisburn wanted to go! Bit by bit he edged nearer the low stone walls until he came smack up against it. The pigs grunted their annoyance at all this noise going on around them and from his higher vantage point, Max could see them gathering near the wall to see what was going on. Gisburn had his hands on the wall as if he were about to sit on it but had changed his mind. However, his mind was made up for him as Charlie made one last, squawking dive towards Gisburn who leant backwards away from the crow. Max could see one fat little leg go up and then the other as he overbalanced over the wall, landing with a squelch in a big pile of mud and pig poo! The pigs, angry at this interruption, started butting him every time he tried to get up and in a matter of seconds there wasn't an inch of Gisburn that wasn't covered in a thick coating of dark brown, gooey, pongy mess.

Max tried to stifle his giggles in case Gisburn heard but Robin, now on the other side of the hedge had no such inhibitions. Max watched as he threw his head back with a loud 'Ha! and then sat on the ground, unable to stand up as he was convulsed with loud and raucous laughter. At this, Charlie flew up towards Robin and over the hedge, landing near Max and fixing him with a beady eye and Max returned the stare warily. He was now worried that Gisburn would see Robin. Gisburn, left in peace now by Charlie was trying to get up in the slippery quagmire of the pig pen but kept slipping back.

Charters had appeared at the door, disturbed by all the noise and with a wave of panic, Max realised he was looking directly at Robin. Quite unexpectedly, he saw Robin get up from the ground and salute Charters in a familiar way and Charters saluted back, his undertaker-like face stretched in a rare grin. Did Charters believe in the legend too then? There was a gloopy noise as Gisburn managed to stand up and start to clear some of the foul-smelling liquid from his eyes. Robin stood back a few paces and took a running jump at the hedge and turned a somersault, landing on his behind but keeping the eggs held up in the air. Robin had another laughing fit before getting up, keeping to the side of the hedge towards the wood. He turned back, juggling the eggs in the air.

'Eggs for breakfast tomorrow – are you coming?' he shouted.

'Scrambled?' replied Max, hardly daring to look.

*

Gisburn plodded his sticky and smelly way to the side door of his manor house, too bruised and too defeated to even show his considerable temper. As Gisburn offered his disgusting jacket on an outstretched arm, Charters gingerly caught it between finger and thumb. As his master slopped dejectedly across the hallway in front of him, a most unservant-like smile spread across Charter's face. That was the most fun he'd experienced in ages!

CHAPTER 17

'Scru-unch!' The gravel sounded loudly underfoot as Joe dropped over the garden wall. There was a united 'Shhh!' from his brother and sister who had avoided the squeaky gate so as not to wake their parents, only to have Joe jump over the wrong part of the wall. They all looked cautiously up to their parents' bedroom window but no light was switched on. After a few seconds, they turned round again and by the light of the moon, made their way to Robbers' Wood.

They were soon joined by two figures running across the field from the direction of the road.

'My mum was up getting a cup of tea' whispered Ethan, 'I thought I'd never get out'.

'I went to bed in my clothes so I was all ready' added Jake.

There was an air of excitement about them. They had each been handed a note by Reverend Rowley telling them to be up at the church at thirty minutes past midnight for a meeting with Robin. Everyone had been very despondent as things weren't happening as quickly as they had hoped and it was now Saturday night – well technically it was the very early hours of Sunday morning – and they were hoping with all their might that Robin had some hope to give them now.

The old door creaked open as Max put his weight against it and they went over to the dais which was dimly lit by a couple of candles at floor level so as not to attract unwanted attention. Robin was sitting there with Rev Rowley but there was no sign of Will. Robin looked up and he raised one eyebrow in his customary fashion.

'I didn't expect you to bring Joe' he said in amusement.

'You try stopping him' said Max with a rueful smile 'but why?'

'We're breaking into Gisburn's crypt tonight and I wasn't sure if he fancied being close up to skeletons and spirits'

There was a collective intake of breath and they grinned at each other, apart from Joe who asked,

'Spirits? You mean...ghosts?' He looked around him quickly and shuddered. Max frowned at Robin who was laughing.

'There won't be any ghosts – just a load of old bones' he said reassuringly, putting his hand on Joe's shoulder which made him jump even more.

'I'm glad you thought I wouldn't be scared Robin' Cait simpered, 'You knew I was old enough to know there are no such thing as ghosts'

'Not exactly' grinned Robin 'I just thought that when you opened your mouth to speak, the ghosts would be more scared of you than you would of them'.

The three older boys stifled their laughter. They could see Cait fold her arms and lower her head like a bull about to charge and didn't want to be subject to one of her tirades! Before she could answer back though, Robin put his hand up for silence.

'As you know, things are not looking too good. If the document proving ownership of the land isn't found by Monday, Gisburn will be given permission to destroy the trees. The one saving grace will be Gisburn's document of ownership of the woods that Will has proved to be forged. He went earlier to the chairman of the committee at his home in Sherburn, the one who seemed to be against Gisburn, in the hope that he can stop it. Even then, it may be too late.' And at this, he exchanged solemn glances with Rowley.

'What do you mean, too late?' asked Max before Robin's answer was cut off by the sound of the church door opening revealing a very hot and flustered Will Scatlock.

'What news Will?' said Robin, standing.

'The worst' he mumbled, coming to a stop in front of the little assembly of people who were all now staring at him wide-eyed.

'He hasn't cut the trees down?' wailed Cait.

'Don't be daft' said Joe 'we could see them when we came to the church.' Although he wasn't entirely sure they were *all* there he thought the wood wouldn't have looked so peaceful if people were chopping the trees down. Cait looked slightly happier until she turned to Will.

'What then? What's the worst?'

'At first light this morning, Gisburn has got an entire army of men to chop all the marked trees down in one day. A day earlier than planned. That's three-quarters of the entire wood!' he explained unnecessarily and went on,

'Something Gisburn said at the last planning meeting made me worry' he nodded across at Robin to indicate he had told him. 'I had my junior partner at the office, Elias Print, make enquiries around all the timber felling firms and no-one was saying anything, they must have been sworn to secrecy on pain of death! Anyway, he got talking to one of them in a pub earlier tonight. He had about a gallon of beer inside him and wasn't in the mood to be secretive. He let Elias in on the secret and told him not to tell anyone, not knowing who he was talking to. He said the 'Big oak tree', which the 'boss' didn't like for some reason, would be the first tree to go.'

At this, even Robin looked worried but this just turned into a steely determination. His pale blue eyes narrowed and his black brows knitted together in a frown.

'What of the Chairman? Did you show him the proof that Gisburn's ownership of the woods is a forgery, made by his grandfather 90 years ago and not an ancient document like he claimed?'

'He was very happy to believe me and has said that the document would help in dismissing Gisburn's plans. He did say though, that it would have to go through all the processes again to satisfy the legal system and even though it might end up with Gisburn's plans being denied permission, until the document turned up showing who the actual owner of the woods was, there was nothing he could do at the moment. He was very sorry...'said Will, looking dejected 'but his hands are tied. He is showing my proof to the committee on Monday but that will be too late. Gisburn can always plead that he thought it was his wood – he doesn't know we have proved the forgery yet. We will be presented with a wood devoid of trees and even if Gisburn doesn't get the planning permission – the wood will be gone.'

These last few words were whispered and silence fell on the listeners. A tear rolled slowly down Joe's cheek.

All of a sudden, Robin's mood changed.

'Come on you unbelievers! We said we would save the wood and we will, however little time we've got. I can feel it in my bones. Talking of which...' and he glanced at Rowley who started to talk hoarsely, as though he too had been upset.

'The church wouldn't give us permission to go into the Gisburn family crypt even though I said I was just making sure everything was okay down there. They said they would have to get the present Mr Gisburn to give his permission. Well of course, that's the *last* thing we wanted, so we are going to have to do it without anyone finding out. Hopefully...' he whispered, raising his eyes to heaven. 'The key was lost before I took over so...'

'We don't need a key' laughed Robin, holding up his dagger and another piece of thin metal. 'Come on, it's out this way' and he led the little band of followers out into the graveyard which was lit only by the eerie, grey-silver light of the moon.

The Gisburn family crypt was an imposing looking stone edifice set in the far corner of the graveyard. The top was merely a large slab of marble set on four plinths with a warlike black marble angel standing on top at the far end, guarding the tomb. The younger members of the band looked at it in alarm while Robin looked amused at their worried faces.

The entrance to the crypt was down five broken and slippery steps at the front as most of the tomb was underground. Robin went down first and after a few minutes of grunting he managed, with the help of Rowley and Will, to unlock it and push the door open a little. The door creaked noisily and everyone glanced round them, worried in case anyone would hear – but there was no one near. Rowley just managed to squeeze his body through and turned on his torch as it was pitch black down there. There were three more steps inside. It also smelt badly of damp soil and decay – Cait wrinkled her nose up and got her handkerchief out to put over her nose and mouth.

There were only four stone coffins in there; two plain stone ones and two more ornate with stone figures lying on top of them. Joe grabbed hold of Max and Cait grabbed hold of Rowley.

They inched forward under the torch's inadequate light until they reached the first coffin.

'Walter Gisburn' read Will 'Can't be Albert's father though, the date's wrong, it's much earlier'.

'The Gisburns haven't been buried in here for years, this is an ancient crypt with their ancestors but it's our only chance.' offered Rowley his torchlight spinning round the walls to look for hiding places for a document.

The walls were bare although there were a few loose stones which Robin and Will examined without finding anything. The floor was examined too and after another five minutes. Robin stood up.

'The coffins it is then.' he said and went over to the nearest one, armed with his dagger ready to prise the top loose.

The children watched in horror as bit by bit, the coffin lid came away from the casket below it and with a superhuman effort, Robin and Will managed to slide it over to reveal what lay below. There wasn't time to look in as there was the most unholy stink emanating from the coffin, it was indescribable but Max thought that must be what death smelt like. The Reverend Rowley glanced sideways at the small figures pressed against the

167

door, their hands up to their faces to try and stop the smell. He turned to Robin with a pleading look.

'Robin…?' he said, indicating the children and Robin suddenly came to his senses.

'Right you lot – outside with you' he ordered. Max suddenly felt as though he were back to his old scared self and was angry as much with himself as with Robin.

'I don't want to go; I want to help. I'm not scared' he said, standing forward but he noticed that the others didn't join in with him.

'I didn't say you were scared Max' replied Robin 'but I brought you all here as lookouts while we broke into the crypt. You're no good looking-out in here – so get yourselves out there and start watching for any sign of movement.'

Robin returned to what he was doing and one by one, the children filed out. Max was last but even though he wanted to join Robin, he was starting to feel sick with the smell so he went slowly up the steps and took up guard at the front of the tomb, overlooking the direction of the town.

Inside, Rowley nodded gratefully at Robin who smiled back. For the next half an hour, no-one inside that cold and ghastly tomb spoke a word as they searched every possible place for the missing document.

Outside though, the children were whispering to each other. They were all sitting at the front of the crypt, facing towards the town, although Ethan and Jake were each posted on the corners in case anyone came from the woods on one side or the fields on the other. One thing was for sure, they were all avoiding looking at the black marble statue of the angel who looked down on them in stony silence. All around them were the graves of the people who had lived in Buckton. Max had been round here with his father, looking at lots of the inscriptions, most of which had worn off. Max's own ancestors were buried here but it certainly didn't make him feel any better knowing that now.

They were just whispering to each other, wondering what would happen if their parents knew they were here when there was a scraping sound behind them. They all jumped up immediately and swung round to look at the slab of stone over the crypt. Everything was black but there, silhouetted against the moon-sky, was the

169

figure of the Black Angel, moving towards them and pointing its sword towards them. The sound of their screams shattered the silence and, as one, they turned back towards the town ready to run for their lives.

Suddenly, they heard the voice of Reverend Rowley

'It's okay children, it's only Robin, he didn't mean to scare you, he just jumped on to the top of the slab. Don't be scared'

His soft and pleading voice stopped them all in their tracks and shaking still with fear, they turned round to see Rowley and Will at the top of the crypt steps while Robin rolled around, shaking, not with fear but laughter, on the top of the tomb.

'They thought I was the avenging angel, come to life!' he spluttered, catching his breath.

Max found this too much. He looked down at Joe who was clinging on to him and then across at Robin, whose laughing fit had turned into chuckles as he sat up.

'That wasn't very grown up was it?' he said.

Robin raised his head in surprise and stared at him before starting to answer.

'No, I must admit…'

Before he had chance to finish what he was saying, a bundle of spitting anger in the form of Cait threw herself on him and started to beat him with her small fists.

'You stupid, childish, idiotic, pathetic excuse for a man. Why did you do that? Why?'

Robin saw the tears rolling down her face and gently took her hand and with his other hand, pulled her chin up so she could see his expression and know that he meant what he was about to say.

'Cait. And the rest of you,' he looked up briefly then back at the small girl still shaking in front of him. 'I didn't mean for one second to scare you. I didn't think about the angel and what you would think if a figure came towards you on the tomb. For doing that, I am truly sorry and I realise I shouldn't have brought you here. Am I childish? Perhaps. Do I not act grown up? Perhaps not…because whether you realise it or not, I have only eighteen summers behind me, apart from the centuries that have stretched on since then and as you may now realise, I am only six years older than the eldest of you. Therefore, hopefully, you can forgive my youthful enthusiasm and misplaced sense of humour. As I said, I shouldn't have brought you here tonight but the truth is, I needed your help. I need you here as proof there are others fighting for the good in this world. That even the young can fight evil as well as the adults. I need you here…as friends.'

There was a silence, only interrupted by Cait's sniffs. Then Max stepped forward, unencumbered now by Joe who was just staring at Robin, his fear forgotten.

'We are proud to be your friends and proud to help you – and we're very glad you are here to help us too.'

The others all murmured their agreement, including Cait who added.

'But if you ever do anything like that again, You Are TOAST!'

Robin grinned at her as he let go of her hand and his eyes looked beyond them, over the graveyard, then back towards the ground in front of him. He stood up slowly, still fixing his gaze on the ground before closing his eyes and throwing his head back towards the moon and stars which suddenly seemed very bright. The children were puzzled but no-one spoke. After a minute, Robin relaxed his tensed body and leaned back against one of the pillars, looking drained. He spoke quietly.

'Now, there is something I have to tell you. There is no point being scared of what you call ghosts and which we call spirits of the woodland, as these were once people like you. Your own families, inhabitants of Buckton and many of my old friends. Even myself. We are going to need help to stop the men chopping down the Wolfshead Tree. Mere men or children maybe won't stop them but they are a superstitious bunch, so perhaps this will.'

He again looked out behind and beyond them into the graveyard and they turned around.

'Now, don't be scared. You have met these characters before.'

Making their way through the gravestones were strange silvery smoke-like apparitions. Nobody moved a muscle as the shapes slowly took a vague human form. One very tall one and one very fat one raised their hands in salute.

'Your outlaw band!' Max whispered, turning to Robin in surprise.

'My friends.' He nodded and waved his own arm in salute to them and addressed the spectral figures seriously.

'Now go to the Wolfshead Tree and keep it safe as long as you can, for all our sakes.'

CHAPTER 18

A murmur was going round the few men brave enough to go near the Wolfshead Tree, even though they were hiding behind undergrowth at least twenty yards away. The foreman knew what it was about; they were going to refuse to work. He looked fearfully towards the Wolfshead Tree and blinked again to make sure he was really seeing the shadowy figures which surrounded the tree on all sides.

He supposed they could start to cut down trees at the other end of the wood but he had strict instructions to cut the Wolfshead Tree down first. Gisburn had drummed it into him how important it was to do that. The foreman had tried to get in touch with Gisburn to tell him what was happening but the mobile phone reception wasn't good so he had sent one of the men, who was glad to get out of that terrible wood, to tell Gisburn himself. Their boss wouldn't be pleased as he had paid them a huge bonus to be here at first light but there was no way he could get the men to do anything while those…Things…were there.

He turned round and looked beyond the small group of men he was with to a larger group, huddled together in a clearing at the edge of the wood. . They had turned tail and run there as soon as they caught sight of the fearsome figures brandishing spectral weapons in front of them. Some of them had even run out of the wood and he doubted they would ever be persuaded back there. He didn't know what to do.

Surely when Gisburn saw what was stopping them working, he would understand, although his dealings with Gisburn so far hadn't exactly shown him to be the understanding sort. He would just have to wait for him to arrive.

*

Max, Cait and Joe were late getting up, much to the surprise of their parents who were used to them rushing out of the house lately as soon as they had wolfed their breakfasts down. Of course, they

176

had no idea that their children had been out all night and had only snatched a couple of hours sleep.

'Ah, you finally made it then?' said Mrs Cooper before she stopped in her tracks at the expression on Max's face. 'What's wrong, what's happened?'

The other two had joined him and now all started to speak at once and their mother couldn't make head nor tail of it but Mr Cooper grasped the seriousness of the situation straight away.

'And they're at Robbers' Wood now you say?'

'Yes' Max almost shouted, 'we have to hurry. They're going to cut all the trees down – and they're going to start with the Wolfshead Tree!'

Their parents looked at one another and nodded.

'We are just going to do a bit of phoning round; you get up there and see what you can do. Here, grab some toast to eat on your way'

Mrs.Cooper opened the front door to find Evie and Eira on their doorstep.

'We saw a lot of men with those yellow hats on running away from the wood' said Eira.

'We think there are lots more still there though, we saw them waiting at the edge of the wood. Can we help?' said Evie.

'Yes' said Mrs Cooper, you can run and tell your mum and dad to find as many townspeople as they can and get up to Robbers' Wood – Now!'

The Cooper children watched them run off back in the direction of their home and they did the thumbs up sign at them, which the twins returned.

Mouths stuffed with toast as it seemed to be ages since they had eaten, the younger Coopers dashed out of the house towards the wood.

*

As the men stood there, afraid to do anything, there was an anguished roar behind them. Gisburn came crashing through the trees in a fury, purple with rage to find that nothing had been done and no trees had been cut down. More importantly, the Wolfshead Tree was still standing. Gisburn marched straight up to the foreman and tried to stand face to face with him although this was harder than he thought as the foreman was a head taller than him.

'What the dickens is going on?!' he shouted. 'I come up here to see how much firewood I can get from that cursed tree and there it is! In all its glory! Why is it still there?' he shouted the last five words slowly as if talking to an imbecile. The foreman didn't take kindly to that. Obviously the man he had sent to tell him, hadn't found him.

'You said to cut the Wolfshead Tree down first before we started any of the others.'

'Yes' Gisburn panted impatiently, 'then why isn't it done?'

'See for yourself' the foreman said and pointed to his left.

Gisburn sprung back a step, his mouth open. Not those damn shadows again! He collected his thoughts quickly. As scared as he was of these otherworldly creatures, if he let the men see it, he would not get the work done today and that meant all his plans would be for nothing. With an effort he made his voice sound steady.

'What are you worried about man? They are smoke and air! They can't harm you.'

He wasn't sure of this fact and knew that the mere existence of these figures was enough to stop the men getting any closer.

'You try telling the men then Mr. Gisburn, they won't listen to me.'

He went off towards the crowd of confused-looking men who didn't look as though they were in any mood to listen and told them they wouldn't receive a penny if they didn't move -now.

Gisburn looked up. It was getting much lighter, the advantage of those first two hours had already gone and his whole scheme was falling apart. They only had so long before they were discovered but it was Sunday and nothing legal could be done till Monday when it would be too late, the woods would have gone.

After grumbling for a while, the men reluctantly started to walk back towards the trees. The grey sky hung over the pitch blackness of the trees and there was an eerie silence now in the air which unsettled the men. They whispered to one another as they walked.

Suddenly, a breeze started up from the stillness and with each step the men took towards the trees, its strength increased. By the time they reached the edge of the wood, it was a raging wind, howling around their ears. Gisburn's piggy eyes opened as wide as they would go and he turned around and saw the men looking at each other, reluctant to go a step further. Gisburn frowned.

'May I remind you that I am paying you three times the normal pay to be here today?'

One of the workmen muttered to himself.

'What was that?' shouted Gisburn to one of the men.

'I said that money isn't everything. There's something strange about those woods and the way that wind just cropped up. I don't fancy going in them.'

Gisburn looked like he might explode. So near and yet so far. What was worse, some of the others were nodding in agreement and a couple of them had even turned to go back.

'Alright, alright' he spluttered then sighed reluctantly, 'Four times your normal wage!'

The men stopped in their tracks and glanced from one to the other. There wasn't one of them who didn't need the money. The first man who had spoken nodded at the men who nodded back in silence.

'All right, four times our wage then' he agreed hesitantly

'Thank goodness for that' grumbled Gisburn and they all marched up to the trees. The wind which had shown no sign of abating now whistled eerily over their heads, the leaves rustling so loudly that it shut out all other noise. Above them, the trees swayed and seemed to part, leaving a clear path to let Gisburn and his army in. They walked forward hesitatingly, expecting something to happen any minute. It did.

As soon as all the men had reached their first objective-the Wolfshead Tree, which Gisburn had expressly said must be cut down first, the trees swayed inwardly now forming a sort of wooden cage around them. They all rushed around trying to prise open the branches blocking their escape but the only way out was towards the Wolfshead Tree, its uppermost branches visible to all.

Into the chaos, a lone figure jumped from the tree and strode towards them. They could see a bow slung over his shoulder and a quiver of arrows on his back. As he came closer, Gisburn could see the mocking smile of none other than Robin Hood. The men stood silently transfixed but Gisburn could see his dreams turning to ashes and collected his thoughts enough to shout,

'He's not real; it's an illusion, a trick of the mind. Onward men, let's do what we came here to do.'

No-one stirred and the echo of Gisburn's words died around him. There was a short silence.

'Oh dear' smiled Robin, raising one puzzled eyebrow 'No-one? No? Well let's try it my way.'

He turned in the direction of the Wolfshead Tree and in a cruel parody of Gisburn's words shouted,

'It's all right, Gisburn isn't real, he's a pathetic trick of the mind' he leant towards Gisburn '...an idiot! Onward men, let's do what we came here to do.'

At that, the shadowy figures made their way towards them. They seemed more solid than they had been. Tall, fat, short, thin: they all came forward so they were facing Gisburn's men. There was no escape. As they advanced on them, swords and staffs at the ready, the men shuffled backwards hoping the trees would open up and let them through. One man started his chainsaw up but lowered it when Robin aimed an arrow at him. The men were caught off guard as arrows flew at them, swords were held at their throats and wooden staffs were used to knock the chainsaws out of reach. The one that was still switched on, skidded, buzzing, across the ground and came perilously close to chopping Gisburn's foot off. Robin leapt with amazing agility onto a lower branch and with his arrow flying true, disarmed some of the workmen. At last, all the chainsaws lay quietly on the mossy floor. There were a few bruises but the workmen looked amazed that they weren't seriously injured.

*

The sun was sending light down in watery beams through the trees. By this time, Gisburn was showing his true colours and cowering in the hollow of one of the trees when he heard something next to his ear. A tapping noise with a sort of hissing in the background. He turned round slowly, hardly daring to breathe to find he was staring into the beady yellow eyes of an enormous crow who was sharing his hiding place. He only had time to wonder why he hadn't scared the crow into flying away when the crow opened its beak. Gisburn waited expectantly.

'Boo!' croaked the crow, right in Gisburn's ear and Gisburn shot out of his hiding place and ended up right in front of the Wolfshead Tree. The shadowy fighting figures had moved back to guard the tree again. Instead of the almost solid figures of a few minutes earlier, he saw that they were dissolving into shimmering outlines. He stood there for a minute transfixed, thinking about this – then his face changed and an evil grin spread across his face. He looked up and saw the sun's rays filtering through the leaves.

'Look, you cowards' he shouted across to his men, 'Look! These men you are fighting are made of fresh air. Dissolving in the sun. Fading in front of your eyes. *You* have the advantage – take it!'

The workmen took a while to process this information but then realised that they were in fact, looking at vague outlines where before they were being attacked by what seemed like real men.

Robin jumped from nowhere it seemed, to stand before Gisburn. His hands defiantly on his waist, he glared at him before turning to his men who were now fast disappearing. Even his own strong magic couldn't make his men appear for too long, especially in the sunlight.

'It is well men; you have done your job and a good one at that. I thank you and I will see you again soon but for now' he looked at the ground sadly then again towards his men 'I dismiss thee'.

Nobody moved for what seemed like minutes then slowly, the remains of Robin's men nodded to him. Some appeared to take their caps off and salute him then, before the eyes of all those assembled, they disappeared into the sun's rays. The trees all bent back to their normal position, to let more of the stronger light through, now there were no spirits to protect.

Forcing his mouth shut with an effort, Gisburn turned to his workmen.

'You see, you're fighting nothing now? There's nothing to stop us!'

He looked across at Robin who was leaning on his bow disconsolately. Gisburn's eyes narrowed as he saw that Robin seemed defeated.

'…and I think we should start with the this accursed oak tree' he said, his mouth twisting into a smile.

Robin continued with his stance for a moment before he stood up straight and faced Gisburn.

'Why not?' he said and graciously swept his arm in front of him, indicating the path to the tree.

Gisburn spluttered in disbelief.

'Is that it? Is that all you have to say? After all your efforts to stop me?'

Robin sighed resignedly.

'It's what you came here for isn't it? My men are gone, how can I stop you?' and he looked sadly upwards before walking back to sit against the tree where the crow had been hiding. The crow flew down and pecked at his ear to cheer him up, which didn't appear to work.

Gisburn couldn't believe his luck. Quickly he shouted,

'Those of you with your chainsaws still working, follow me.' and with that, he leant forward to pick up a chainsaw himself and with his men trailing reluctantly behind, he made his way to the Wolfshead Tree.

CHAPTER 19

Meanwhile, at the Cooper's farmhouse, Mrs Cooper was pulling on her coat. The children all ran in at full speed. Max looked across at his dad who had been studying something on the table.

'What's the rush Max?' he said now, 'has something happened?'

'We can't get into the wood, it was weird, the trees wouldn't let us through.'

Mr.Cooper looked puzzled.

'I can't explain it. It's like they were either trying to keep us out or the chainsaw men in. Almost as if the trees were living things with minds capable of thinking. Maybe they were trying to protect the Wolfshead Tree?' Max finished, now believing everything he had heard about the wood being enchanted. 'We have to hurry though.'

Joe blurted out the story of the crypt but as the other two held their breath in case they were found out, he whispered it was 'Roly poly who had gone in the crypt to find the deeds' Max and Cait breathed a sigh of relief.

'So the deeds weren't in the crypt?' said Mr. Cooper quietly to himself, 'I wonder…? I've been studying this poem and I think it may be referring to this farmhouse.

The children, who were on their way out again, stopped in their tracks and turned round open-mouthed.

'You see, the stream runs nearby, this is Hartshead Farm as deer used to roam freely in the woods that contained this building. We thought casks –'where only the casks lie' – meant caskets or coffins. Yet many years ago this was a coaching inn, the last stop before Buckton and I wondered if the poem meant wine or ale casks and 'below' might refer to our cellar. There aren't any left now, as you know there's nothing down there now but boxes of our own but still…'

'What's the Ancient Tree's namesake then or the brimstone and stuff?' asked Cait.

'That's what set me thinking' smiled their Dad, 'I've looked at our own deeds to this house and Hartshead Farm used to be called The Great Oak Tavern. The Wolfshead Tree is a giant oak.'

There was silence for a moment then everything seemed to happen at once.

'I will take Cait and Joe to the woods, maybe we can do something to help and Max can help you search in the cellar' said Mrs Cooper.

'Come on Max' said his Dad' There's no time to lose!'

Max followed his father as he rummaged in the back of a drawer, eventually holding up an enormous iron key for the cellar door. Mr. Cooper explained as they ran into the hallway. 'Our family has been here for hundreds of years. The name Cooper mean maker of barrels or casks which is what probably happened. The Coopers made the casks for the ale and used them for the tavern. Quite often two trades were combined and the bigger barn at the back was probably the cooperage where they made the barrels.'

The key was not turning. It hadn't been used for a year or so and was too stiff to turn. Max waited impatiently while his father gave it a turn with both hands and suddenly, the enormous wooden door creaked open. They exchanged glances and as his father reached for the light switch; they went slowly down the uneven stone steps and into the gloom of the dimly-lit cellar.

They flinched as cobwebs stuck to their faces and watched large spiders run away from the people who were intruding on their space.

'Now, the poem again' said Mr.Cooper, fishing the piece of paper from his pocket and squinting at it. 'They wait next to Brimstone, Salt and Fire. We know where the fire is at least'.

'Do we?' asked Max, looking around in vain for a fireplace.

'Yes, it's there – behind all those boxes' and he pulled an apologetic face at Max.

Eventually, after manhandling all the boxes out of the way regardless of what was in them, they uncovered the fire and Mr. Cooper stepped inside the inglenook to feel around the sooty walls of the chimney.

'I can't feel anything unusual. No loose stones or ledges.' he cried out in exasperation. 'Come and help me then!'

Max just stood in front of the fire, not even attempting to help. A calm feeling had come over him and could hear Robin's voice inside his head saying 'Think…Think!'

Almost as if her were being guided there, he walked over to the left-hand side of the huge fireplace and after sweeping more cobwebs and dust from the wall, he saw a recess, a small shelf going back into the wall. He reached his hand towards what looked like a small wooden door at the back of it. It had a hole in it, big enough to put his finger through. There was a lock just underneath the hole.

Dad? Where would the salt have been kept when this place was built? Next to the fire?'

'Of course!' laughed his father, suddenly remembering. They used to keep salt dry in a little cupboard next to the fire. Brimstone had to be kept dry too – and ventilated'

'Like this little cupboard?' asked Max pulling on the tiny door which probably hadn't been opened for hundreds of years. 'Blast! I think it's locked'

'It would be. Very valuable in those days was salt' muttered Mr. Cooper and suddenly shot out of the fireplace, giving Max a big, sooty hug on the way upstairs to the kitchen to find something open the small door. At the same time, Max's eyes opened wide with realisation and he was on his father's heels in a rush to get to the top. He then dashed up to his bedroom, leaving a trail of dust up the wooden stairs. Throwing the door open he flew over to the chest where he kept his most treasured possessions. Right at the bottom was an old toffee tin which Max had used to keep the smaller objects in when he was much younger. Wrenching it open, he pulled out some rusty keys on a metal ring. Running down again at top speed he nearly collided with his father who came racing out of the kitchen. Mr Cooper held up a screwdriver and a hammer. Max smiled at him and held up the keys.

'You don't think...?' spluttered his father.

'Only one way to find out' answered Max who was already pushing past his father and down into the cellar again.

'But how...?' asked Mr.Cooper who was almost rendered speechless by the keys and the effort of running.

'They were in my 'Treasure' box. I dug them up about four years ago when I was looking for buried treasure. They were buried at the back of the barn you were talking about, where they made barrels'

Mr.Cooper smiled at his son. Where was the shy boy now who had no confidence in himself? He felt so proud of his boy. Even more so when one key, which was brown with rust, opened the door at the first go. He watched Max reach in and carefully pull something out.

'It's another treasure box' smiled Max wryly as they stared at an old square metal box. It was very heavy.

'Made of lead I expect or at least lead-lined. I don't suppose it's open' his father said, looking sadly at yet another keyhole on the front of the box.

'No' said Max tugging at it 'but there's this!' and handing the box to his father, he held up the strange-shaped key which had been with the salt cupboard key.

'It could be it,' he told Max, 'try it!'

Max gingerly put the key in the lock, terrified that it wouldn't fit. He thought his father's hammer might come in handy after all but here was a slight click and two pairs of hands frantically pulled at the box lid. Inside was a yellow piece of paper rolled up and tied with a ribbon. No, not paper. It felt quite stiff to touch, like parchment. Taking it over to stand under the dull light of the only light bulb in the cellar, Max and his father began to read the words that were written there in old-fashioned copperplate writing. As they read, a smile touched both their faces.

CHAPTER 20

Made bold by the disappearance of Robin's men and the apparent surrender of Robin himself, the men made their way up to the Wolfshead Tree, the chainsaws that were undamaged were held in front of them. They were led by a delighted Gisburn.

Behind him trailed a very disappointed Charters who had come up with a flask of coffee laced with brandy for his master. Charters had desperately wanted to see him defeated today. He quickly took a swig out of Gisburn's flask to calm him down. He couldn't believe that the Wolfshead Tree, which had stood here when his great, great, great grandfather had walked through the woods, was going to be cut down.

Gisburn was looking uncomfortable. He could hear sounds in the forest and looked to where Robin had been standing a couple of minutes earlier but he had vanished now. He thought, if he listened carefully, that he could hear the sounds of undergrowth being trampled underfoot. Gradually though, that sound was accompanied by a low humming noise. Gisburn stopped in his tracks to listen more carefully and noticed some of the workmen had stopped too and were looking around them.

Suddenly some of the workmen fell back as Mrs Cooper with Cait and Joe appeared through the branches and came into the clearing. With them were Ethan and Jake and they all stepped forward at once, a defiant look in each pair of eyes.

Gisburn smiled to himself. If this was the rescue party, then who did they think they were scaring? Not him, that's for sure. Yet the humming noise continued and before his very eyes, people appeared from between the trees, walking en masse towards himself and his men. At the front of them were Evie and Eira, like warrior princesses with their long curly hair flowing, leading all the townsfolk to the woods. Just behind them were Will Scatlock and the Reverend Rowley - and there beside them, grinning like a fox who has just found his prey, was Robin Hood.

Too late, Gisburn realised the hum had been people talking. Hundreds of them as they marched up to the woods. Hundreds of the people of Buckton – all here to stop him cutting down the wood and especially this cursed Wolfshead Tree that stood before him. Gisburn felt like screaming. So near and yet so far. He watched helplessly as the townspeople sat down all around the Wolfshead Tree. The children climbed the tree and some of the younger men and women climbed into the branches of surrounding trees.

Silence had descended and now nearly all the people were facing Gisburn with hostility in their eyes. Almost unnoticed by him two small figures had walked up to where he stood with a confused look on his face. A small but defiant voice piped up from below him.

'You are never going to cut Robbers' Wood or the Wolfshead Tree down' announced Cait.

'No!' confirmed Joe next to her.

'You can see that all the townspeople have turned out to support us. They are here to stop your wicked scheme.'

'Yes!' affirmed Joe.

'So you may as well go back and take your men with you cos you are FINISHED here!' Cait shouted.

'Yes!!' screamed Joe enthusiastically and started dancing about, much to the amusement of the onlookers.

Gisburn looked surprised at the ferocity of these children but gradually recovered himself, putting an imperious look on his flabby little face.

'May I remind you all that this wood belongs to me and I can do what I want with it? My lawyer will tell you as much.' he said, looking uncertainly at Will, 'Now let me through.'

Gisburn grabbed the chainsaw from the startled man behind him and started to pick his way through the people who tried to grab him to stop him.

'I don't think so Gisburn!' came Will's voice over the general murmuring. 'I have here proof that your document of ownership was forged and so the land doesn't belong to you at all. You're nothing but a cheat and a liar!'

Will waved the piece of paper in the air and there were smiles spreading around the crowd.

Gisburn thought for a moment then smiled his twisted smile.

'Then give me proof of who it does belong to then Scatlock because until then, being the Lord of the Manor so to speak, I think you will find the courts will find in my favour for any claim on the land. In the absence of the documents you need, even if this wood and that darned tree isn't cut down today, I will make personally sure that it won't be long before it is!'

There was a discontented murmur from the crowd and Scatlock hesitated for a moment but it was all Gisburn needed to know that he was right.

'No document eh Scatlock? What a shame. No proof at all that this wood belongs to the people? So you haven't won after all.' And Gisburn grinned that awful grin as he looked over the heads of the crowd, making Charters wince and jump away from his master.

In the silence that followed there was a heavy rustling of branches and then running footsteps were heard. The two red-faced figures of Max and his father appeared in front of Gisburn. As his father went to join Mrs Cooper, Max strode up to Gisburn, his head held high.

'Here Gisburn' he spat the words out 'here is the document. The document that you hoped would never see the light of day. Here is the proof that this land does not and never has belonged to you. You have tried to cut our wood down – yes, OUR wood - and I will personally see to it that you will not go unpunished!'

Amongst the happy and surprised people of Buckton, Max's father and mother exchanged proud glances.

Gisburn stepped towards Max but Max was too light on his feet and sprang backwards. He turned towards Robin and walked over with the deeds held out in front of him.

'Here Robin, you take these' he said.

Robin bowed very low, taking off his cap as he did so in a gesture of respect.

'You have done so well' he smiled 'you and your friends'

He looked around at Cait and Joe, then further back towards Ethan, Jake, Evie and Eira, who all put their fists in the air to acknowledge Robin, like ancient warriors to their chieftain.

'People of Buckton' he continued, 'without the intervention of these children, these trees would no longer exist.'

Robin leant forward and whispered in Max's ear as loud applause broke out and smiling faces could be seen all around them. Robin stopped whispering and they all surged forward to congratulate him and his friends. Max didn't even feel embarrassed as he would have a few weeks ago. Robin took the document and immediately turned to the Reverend Rowley.

'These are for you I believe' he smiled, adding the words of the poem, 'To be delivered up by God's mercy to the Holy Church, then order will be restored to Buckton and its people'

Rowley took the parchment from Robin, unrolled it, frowning at first to try and put the words into modern day English so everyone could understand. He found the most important words at the bottom of a lot of words he couldn't make out – but these, he could. He began to read them out in a loud voice.

'The area of Buckton known as Robbers' Wood, which contains the Ancient Oak, shall belong to the Church of Buckton and for ever after, through them, to Buckton and its people, to use unchanged as common land and grazing for their animals and for their leisure as the church and the people think fit. This being the last and final word.'

A great cheer erupted from everyone and strangers hugged other strangers who would soon become friends through this extraordinary day.

Unnoticed by any of the people present, Gisburn who at the reading of the deed had looked helplessly down and seeing the chainsaw still there in his hands had crept slowly towards the Wolfshead Tree. The people had abandoned their vigil now it was safe. As the noise of celebration quietened down, Gisburn saw his chance. As more of the people started to notice where he was, he threw his porky little head back and laughed a horribly evil laugh.

'Do you think I care about an old bit of paper?' he shrieked across the heads of the increasingly agitated townspeople. 'Do you think I actually care what happens to this wood or the people of Buckton? This Tree has been a curse on my family for hundreds of years. Just as we think we are getting our own way – that…that…Devil' he spluttered, pointing at Robin 'pops up out of

203

nowhere and changes our fortunes. Always, throughout the generations, he always gets the better of us. Just because we happened to kill someone he loved. Well – NO MORE! There will be no chance for him to come back to these woods – no more humiliation and 'righting wrongs'! I have had enough!' He screamed like a banshee, his eyes almost popping out of his head.

'He's lost it' whispered Cait smugly to Joe, who nodded wisely in agreement.

Suddenly though the smug smiles turned to looks of horror as Gisburn started the chainsaw up and with a lightning reaction which belied his size, he stuck the blade straight into the waiting trunk of the Wolfshead Tree.

Everyone started to surge towards the tree again but tripped over each other in their panic. There were people all over the clearing and still Gisburn cut even deeper into the trunk. Over the general clamour came a roar that stopped everyone in their tracks.

'GISBURN!!'

Gisburn turned his head round, a maniacal grin still on his face. His expression slowly changed into one of apprehension as he saw Robin standing feet apart, his bow drawn back to its full extent and aimed directly at him. His eyes closed but he couldn't let go of the chainsaw, it was as if his hands were glued to it. There was a Whoosh and a ripping of the air then suddenly the arrow made contact with the whirring chainsaw, propelling it out of the trunk. Bits of broken chainsaw blade and arrow flew all around Gisburn who stood there empty-handed and there was a final thud as the lethal weapon fell onto the floor, as useless as the gibbering Gisburn was now.

A great cheer echoed around the forest from tree to tree and someone shouted 'Three cheers for Robin, Hip hip…'

'Hurray, Hurray, HURRAY!'

Robin smiled and nodded at them all and walked up to the Wolfshead Tree. Everyone had started to turn back for Buckton now, their job done. The workmen, shamed by the townspeople's' show of solidarity, walked off hurriedly back down the field to Cheetingham Manor to collect their transport and drive out of there as quickly as they could.

Gisburn himself plodded slowly towards the edge of the wood, his head down and a look of absolute defeat on his face. Charters started to follow him but looked at the others going down to Buckton to celebrate and decided to join them. He couldn't work for Gisburn again, no matter how much he paid him. He would retire to his little cottage near the sea.

Max looked at Gisburn and started to feel sorry for him but realised just in time that people who try to double cross others without any regard for those peoples' feelings did not deserve his sympathy. He turned round to look at Robin who was standing under the branches of the Wolfshead Tree. Max's sister, brother, cousins and friends came up to join him, slapping his back and hugging each other in delight, they too turned their eyes to Robin. Raising his bow high above his head, he saluted them all and they all cheered wildly and waved back at him before following their families back to Buckton.

Max lingered for a moment staring at Robin who grinned back at him with a last wave, then joined his friends, trying his best not to turn back towards Robin as he just knew he wouldn't be there. He put a brave expression on his face and reluctantly marched down away from the Wolfshead Tree and out of the woods.

They could hear uproarious laughter and to their left as they emerged from the wood, they saw Gisburn running across the field back to his home. He had his arms up over his head and was waving them around like a windmill. Max eventually saw the cause of this action was the malevolent crow Charlie, who was flying round Gisburn's head and pecking at him to make sure he went straight home and kept well away from the wood.

CHAPTER 21

It was a fine, summer's evening as five children set off towards the wood from the farmhouse. It was two days after Gisburn's defeat and they had just come from Max's thirteenth birthday party so he was now officially a teenager and felt much more grown up. He knew that had nothing to do with his age though but more what he had gone through in the past few weeks. He had to grow up quickly and the old Max who was unsure of everything had gone now, to be replaced with a confident boy who knew he would always be on the side of right. He now knew that most problems were not insurmountable if you put your mind to it.

He thought about the extraordinary time he had experienced with Robin, his brother and sister, who he tolerated much more than before, and his friends. Also he looked at his parents with a new respect, as he did with Will and Reverend Rowley. Everything had worked out very well in the end and Robbers' Wood was now officially safe- the charter they had found in the cellar was the reason for that. It belonged to Buckton, its people and its church and nothing would change that now.

Gisburn had been threatened with prosecution for fraud but had managed to get out of it with his 'friends in high places'. Max thought it was a good job he had those friends at least as he certainly didn't have any in Buckton. He still had to pay a huge fine straight to the 'Conservation of Robbers' Wood Society' which was dedicated to looking after the wood and the animals, birds, insects and flowers within it. Gisburn would always find some other trouble to cause but for now he was being careful and was holed up in Cheetingham Manor, hoping things would soon cool down.

As they all approached the clearing where the Wolfshead Tree was, Joe ran ahead of them shouting for Robin. Max held back as the others joined Joe, shouting out Robin's name and calling for him to come out. After a few minutes, Joe turned round with a frown on his face.

'I think he must be asleep'

'Yes Joe, he is' replied Max and something in the tone of his voice made them all turn round to him with questioning looks on their faces.

'He's gone back to sleep for as long as it takes. Ten years, fifty years, one hundred years or more? Until the next time Buckton, its people or the woods are in danger.'

He was aware of the tears rolling down Joe's face and he knew he himself felt the same but he must be strong now. Robin had taught him that.

'He can't have, he wouldn't just leave us like that' cried Cait, her own face screwed up, trying not to cry.

'He's playing a joke on us' said Ethan, looking round uncertainly

'He would have said something' said Jake, shaking his head.

'He did say something' whispered Max, his voice suddenly hoarse with emotion 'when I handed him the charter, he whispered to me then. I didn't really take it in until a few minutes later but then I realised he was going. I'll tell you what he said'

They all watched Max intently, waiting for Robin's words.

'He said " You have all done well. I am proud of you and you should be proud of yourselves. My work here is done now. Please give my good wishes to all my little friends with the hope that we may meet sometime in the future."'

Max stopped and watched their reactions. They all bent their heads to look at the ground. After a minute or two of complete silence, Cait said in a breezy manner which was a little too forced,

'That willow den wants rebuilding further down the wood; we need it to provide a good shelter'

Ethan and Jake nodded slowly in agreement and they all trailed down towards the willow. After glaring at Max for a minute, expecting him to say something else, Joe sadly followed the others.

With a last look at the Wolfshead Tree, standing there, solid and immovable, Max went after them all. He smiled to himself as he went as he hadn't told them the last words Robin had said to him and him alone. He had smiled as he whispered,

'Max, you would have been a very good addition to my band of outlaws. Stay strong.'

And Max knew that he would.

The trees started to rustle loudly and the air itself around him seemed to change. The leaves whispered amongst themselves, voices echoing over generations. Max could feel Robin's presence as strongly as ever and he knew that even if they couldn't see him, Robin would always be here, guarding these woods.

Joe turned round, a small figure in the distance but his voice carried up to Max.

'Okay, I'm on my way' and he ran to join the others, watched unbeknown to him, by a pair of beady little yellow crow-eyes, hiding in the hollow of a large tree trunk. Standing guard over the entrance – until the next time.

THE END

Printed in Great Britain
by Amazon